RAC

LOOKING FOR THE BEST

The BBC 'Breakaway' holiday guide

Roger Macdonald

Published for the Royal Automobile Club
by RAC Motoring Services Limited
in association with Hogg Robinson Travel
by arrangement with BBC Publications,
a division of BBC Enterprises Ltd

First published 1986 by RAC Motoring Services Ltd
RAC House Lansdowne Road Croydon CR9 2JA
Copyright © Royal Automobile Club 1986
Published by arrangement with BBC Publications, a division
of BBC Enterprises Ltd

Designed by Laurence Bradbury
   assisted by Rachel Foster
Cartography by MJL Cartographics
Picture research by Anne-Marie Ehrlich
Typeset by SX Composing
Printed and bound by Springbourne Press Ltd, Essex

ISBN 0 86211 055 6

Every effort has been made to ensure that the information given
in this publication is accurate and up to date. However, the
RAC cannot accept responsibility for errors or ommissions, or for
changes in regulations, prices or general conditions.

Cover illustrations front left Neuschwanstein
                   front right Hadrian's Villa, Tivoli
                   back – Seychelles

Acknowledgments
J. Allan Cash 4, 12, 45, 63, 78, 84, 94, 126, 128
BBC Hulton Picture Library 60
Laurence Bradbury 6, 119, 134
Bridgeman Art Library 13
CIT 26
Richard Cooke 138–9
Robert Estall 111, 150
E T Archive 19, 64
Mary Evans Picture Library: Raspé, Magasin Pittoresque
   1867, 14
Sonia Halliday & Laura Lushington 33, 81
Robert Harding Picture Library 5, 34, 120
Image in Industry 159
Indian Government Tourist Office 75
R. Macdonald 53
Mandarin Hotel 144
Mansell Collection 46; 49, Anderson; 95 Nuno Goncalves,
   Lisbon Museum
Tony Morrison 155
National Motor Museum, Beaulieu 8 bottom
N.H.P.A. 141; 142, Robinson
P & O Cruises 115
Photobank   Title page, 130, 133, Peter Baker; 96,
   Jeanetta Baker
Planet Earth 149 Seaphot Walter Deas
Popperfoto 82 top
Ritz Hotel (P. Habans) 57
Seychelles Tourist Board 148, back cover
SNCF-French Railways 67, 68
Spanish National Tourist Office 40, 42, 47
Spectrum 18, 25, 73, 77, 79, 87, 108, 112, 125
Swiss National Tourist Office 28
Ullstein Bilderdienst 137
Venice-Simplon-Orient Express Photo Library 62
Werner Forman Archive 21 right
Stuart Windsor 54, 55
Zefa front cover left, Goebel: front cover right, D. Pittius; 3;
   8 top, M. Fugere; 17; 21 left, H. Kraft; 22, K. D. Fröhlich;
   24, Starfoto; 31, Kotoh; 37, Starfoto; 39; 42; 50, Kotoh; 51,
   Eric Carle; 70, Orion Press; 72, E. Bleicher; 74, E. G. Carle;
   82 bottom, Fritz Bergman; 93; 99, Everts; 102, M. Wilkins;
   105, K. Schulz; 106; 122, F. Damm; 145, Starfoto; 146, Orion
   Press; 147, Hoffman Burchardi; 153, K. Scholtz; 154, D. Doltz;
   156, Schlenker.

CONTENTS

CONTENTS

CONTENTS

INTRODUCTION

This is a provocative book. There are, after all, no absolutes in travel: attempts to examine it, consumer fashion, as though it were a washing machine, have always proved a dismal failure. Individual tastes vary so sharply, individual holidays differ so much, that no one can really be certain of discovering someone else's ideal.

But then successful travel is largely a matter of experience, if only all too often the feeling of having arrived too late, when one's fellow tourists, however unintentionally, have tampered with the natural and unspoilt environment simply by their presence: when even the natives say sadly, 'you should have been here last year'.

It is with considerable trepidation, therefore, that many of the places are mentioned at all, because a significant increase in the number of visitors would rob them of their charm. Pérouges, Tivoli (not the Copenhagen pleasure park), Ronda (no connection with a Welsh Valley), and Kichwa Tembo would never be the same again; El Hierro, Hvar, Saba, Cancun, Kudahithi and the Andaman Islands would be ruined for ever.

Some of these places are a sensible drive from Britain; others, not even a sensible flight from anywhere. What they all offer in common is a reasonable standard of comfort on arrival, for this is not a book for the backpacker, or the travelling sado-masochist; it assumes that most people want a holiday, not an endurance test. Quite unashamedly, the emphasis is on sunshine, sand and seeing things, because the vast majority want precisely those.

It is also a book which in some ways reflects the age we live in: the age of the golden handshake, of buying on credit and spending more than we can afford, of travel one-upmanship. For those who are prepared to blow their savings, or to borrow, recklessly, from the bank, for the proverbial holiday of a lifetime, this is an attempt to ensure that they do not return disappointed. It describes, therefore, the realities of a trip on Concorde or the QE2 or the Orient Express; of some of the true spectacles of the world, the Grand Canyon, the Siena Palio and the Rio Carnival, and what it is like to stay in the great hotels, such as the Mandarin in Hong Kong, the Ritz in Paris, or The Beverley Hills, or in Princess Margaret's villa; or even how to rent a château all to yourself.

This is not simply an exercise in self-indulgence for the idle (and not so idle) rich. A large number of the places included in this book can be reached by a day or two's motoring, or by a cheap charter flight. Many of the selected hotels are still sensibly priced and represent outstanding value. The assessment of Mediterranean beaches is of equal relevance whether you are living in luxury or exercising stringent economies.

Provocative, then, this book may be, but also in the sense of provoking travel to some places that were previously just names on the map, to others whose very existence had hitherto been unknown. There is no substitute for going to see for yourself. To help you on your way, here is an entirely subjective choice of the best in travel – unless of course, you know better...

In the 18th century, the Grand Tour was the finishing touch to a Young Gentleman's education. The Tour, lasting a year or more, usually went through Paris to Italy, then home through Switzerland. With a knowledge of Classical architecture and a collection of statues, a Gentleman was ready to rebuild the family home in Italian style, with echoes, perhaps, of the Piazza della Signoria, Florence.

Even in a Rolls Royce Phantom, a Motoring Tour in 1927 rarely went further than the Riviera.

CHAPTER 1

THE MOTORING GRAND TOUR

A steam omnibus made the first recorded motor coach tour, a six day extravaganza which began in Paris on July 11, 1898, meandered through France and Switzerland, and ended in Aix-les-Bains six days later. Luggage was carried on the roof, but the coach was open at the sides, less of a problem than one might expect, as the average speed on the flat was a mere ten miles an hour. According to an advertisement for the tour, the cost was 180 francs, and six hours a day were to be spent 'in actual autocaring'. Exactly how the passengers were expected to retrace their steps to Paris remains a mystery; presumably it was by train.

Coach travel became more comfortable after the First World War. In 1920 Motorways of London began a luxury service between Calais and Cannes, using a pair of specially built bodies on a military truck chassis. They were so wide that there was room for a dozen swivel armchairs inside, plus a kitchen and a toilet. Motorways made quite a success of long distance travel: by 1924, they were offering coach holidays to Morocco and, in 1935, they were the first to brave the Bolsheviks and take a coach party into Soviet Russia.

For the individual motorist, however, the Grand Tour remained a romantic, but impractical journey. Cars were noisy, uncomfortable and unreliable. When individual motoring tours began to be sold by travel agents in 1903, the prudent gentleman motorist took along a skilled mechanic. A spare can of petrol was quite essential, as petrol stations were many miles apart and kept the same hours as shops. The earliest pneumatic tyres tended to wear out after about 400 miles, even on the best roads, which were few and far between.

The pioneer motorist tended, therefore, to travel quite modest distances and to regard a trip over the Alps, into Italy, as the height of daring. However, he did have some advantages over his modern counterpart. Unless he was travelling as far as the Austro-Hungarian Empire, unlikely by car, he did not need a passport. His money went a great deal further than his vehicle: with the City of London calling the tune in the stock exchanges of the world, the British pound was, literally, as good as gold. It was worth a staggering five US dollars, 20 German marks, and 25 French francs.

Travel by car had one great advantage then: there were few other vehicles using the roads. The construction of inter-city motorways did not begin until 1923, in Italy, but gathered momentum under Mussolini so that by 1932, 330 miles of autostrada were already open to traffic. But they were not dual carriageway, unlike the German autobahn, which were started in 1931 and pushed ahead by Hitler with such vigour that when the war came, 2,300 miles of German motorway had been completed, with hard shoulders and proper cambers, so speeds of 100mph were quite feasible.

The Motoring Grand Tour, unlike the Grand Tourer or GT model that capitalised on its name, is a modern concept in the practical sense. The roads between the Fascist motorways were so indifferent that to reach the south of Italy from London (including the hoisting of your car on and off a

Channel ferry) could take four or five days. On a similar journey to Spain you ran the risk of being attacked by brigands or running into the midst of the Civil War. It is only since the completion of the motorway spine from just outside Calais down the east coast of Spain and to the very toe of Italy, that sustained, long-distance motoring has become a reality, taking advantage of Alpine road tunnels and all-night garages. The only remaining obstacles are the cost and, possibly, fatigue.

The two new Grand Tours described are a feasible proposition for a three-week holiday, by the enthusiastic motorist with a powerful car, using a combination of fast motorways and scenic routes, with long travelling days interspersed with periods of local touring. The choice of interesting places to visit is, unashamedly, subjective, but the places chosen include some of the best scenery in Europe, some of the most beautiful buildings, and some colourful occasions bordering on the bizarre. It is, of course, not possible to be in the right place at the right time throughout the tour without spending far longer than three weeks abroad; visitors, especially those who fly and rent a car, may prefer to sample only a few of the proposed destinations, to combine parts of the two tours, or to divert to other places of interest. The secret is to have something to change: planning a tour is never easy when starting with a blank piece of paper.

However, planning *is* essential, and not only the documentation for the car and its passengers, servicing, spare parts and insurance. Each day's itinerary should really be mapped out in detail, complete with intermediate stops and overnight stays. Few of the selected places to visit are, in any way, suitable for taking pot-luck on hotels, especially in high season. If you have any thoughts of staying in even some of the selected hotels, advance booking – months, not weeks ahead – is almost essential. In large towns or cities, pinpointing the hotel locations in street maps in advance may save hours of frustration at a point when you are physically and mentally least able to cope. There is nothing worse than being unable to find your hotel, or discovering that there is 'no room at the inn' at a whole succession of places.

The most common error is to over-estimate the distance you can drive in one day. These new Grand Tours are not recommended in three weeks for families with young children or for passengers near retirement, or for unenthusiastic drivers – unless of course the routes are joined at some intermediate point following a flight out, and probably a flight back. Even those who feel capable of the entire trip will do well to resist the temptation to drive any substantial distance on more than two consecutive days, because fatigue becomes cumulative, and will certainly spoil your appreciation of the places you are striving to reach.

Older children, who may often last the pace much better than their parents, can become increasingly resentful and uncooperative as the holiday progresses. One possible answer is to involve them as closely as possible in the planning, on where, for example, to stop for a meal or overnight, so that they feel they are being treated as adults and – though do not count on it – respond accordingly.

Apart from driving too far too fast, touring holidays flounder most frequently under the pressure of arriving at and leaving hotels. For overnight stops, always pack the barest minimum of essentials separately, so that heavier baggage can be left in the car. However tempting, never plan to depart early in the morning; it causes more rows than everything else put together. Always check by telephone that the hotel at your next destination is expecting you.

Build in a substantial midpoint stop on every long travelling day. When you arrive in an area (such as the wooded outskirts of Paris, the Bay of Naples or southern Spain) with several places to see, find a hotel within easy reach of all of them, and use this as a base to avoid more packing and unpacking. If you have any spare time, build it into this part of the holiday to make a real break from continual travelling.

THE MOTORING GRAND TOUR

EUROPE

ATLANTIC OCEAN

MEDITERRANEAN SEA

London
Folkestone
Boulogne
Calais
Chantilly
Chartres
Paris
Blois
Amboise
Chaumont
Beaufort-en-Vallée
Chambord
Montsoreau
Chenonceaux
Chinon
Montresor
Azay-le-Rideau

Amsterdam
Bruges
Marburg
Würzburg
Heidelberg

Interlaken
Venice
Lyon
Geneva
Grasse
Portofino
Sestri Levante
St Paul
Forte dei Marmi
Marseille
Diano Marina
Pisa
Pamplona
Carcassonne
Monaco
Florence
Nice
San Gimignano
Rosas
Juan les Pins
Siena
Cadaques
Estartit
Cannes
Gerona
Aiguablava
St Raphael
Rome
Lloret del Mar
Palamos
Castelldefels
S'Agaro
Barcelona
Tossa del Mar

Gulf of Kotor
Dubrovnik
Rimini
Split
Budva
Sveti Stefan
Vesuvius
Naples
Pompeii
Capri

Monchique
Cordoba
Javea
Valencia
Minorca
Seville
Majorca
Granada
Ibiza
Faro
Ronda
Benidorm
Formentera
Albufeira
Nerja
Villajoyosa
Sagres
Almunecar
Malaga
Gibraltar
Marbella
Ceuta

0   250   500
Kilometres

AMSTERDAM

An unsurpassed network of canals, more than twice as many as Venice, gives Amsterdam its unique charm. This is the home of the hoisting hook, where moving house often meant hiring a boat not a furniture van, and where a canal frontage was so expensive that houses were designed pencil-thin, many with rooms leading one into another. They were built to lean outwards, deliberately, so that hoisting goods and chattels would not scar the walls.

Paradoxically, Amsterdam is best seen not by boat, but on foot. The glass-topped boat tours, with unimaginative recorded commentaries, always following the same route at the same precise pace, convey little of the true flavour of the city. Above all this is a place for improvisation, for wandering without a time schedule. Only then can you appreciate the rows of houseboats, some of which provide little cottage industries, the delightful intersections of canals and bridges, with a cluster of stalls offering fish and flowers and bric-à-brac from dawn to dusk, and the cosy cafés where you can drink a mug of Dutch gin and meet people who are not clutching a guidebook.

Alternatively you can get on your bike, or, in reality, someone else's, for renting bicycles in Holland is a huge industry. But be warned: the Dutch all fancy themselves as embryonic racing cyclists and are frequently guilty of violently anti-social behaviour, crowding you with their elbows and making sudden, unannounced turns. Make sure your brakes are in good order.

But at least on a bike you have access to many of Amsterdam's 650-odd bridges, which were, certainly, never designed for motor cars. One of the narrowest, and the most famous, is the Skinny Bridge, called, for some obscure reason, after two British ladies, who were Skinny in name but not, apparently, in appearance.

The dam that gave Amsterdam its name was built (in what became Dam Square) on the Amstel River in 1275, raising the water

Bridge over the Singel Canal

level and giving its fishermen and merchants easier access to the sea. This led to the great Dutch trading tradition and the rise of Dutch seapower. In the first half of the 17th century, Holland established a colonial empire for the commercial activities of its East and West India Companies; Amsterdam became Europe's leading financial centre. It was from Amsterdam that Henry Hudson left for his odyssey to America, setting out from the Tower of Tears in his tiny ship the *Half Moon* in 1609. He gave his name to the Hudson River and founded the settlement of New Amsterdam, which became, in time, New York.

The 17th century was the golden age of the Netherlands of which Holland is a part, whose increasingly affluent merchants sought social prestige through the patronage of art. It was as the result of the encouragement and financial help of the Six family that Rembrandt Harmenszoon van Rijn, the son of a poor miller, settled in Amsterdam and painted most of his great works. But even Rembrandt's pictures were not above economic considerations. His most famous painting

The Night Watch, portrays a group of officials of a City Guild whose faces live on for posterity because they agreed to pay 100 guilders apiece for the privilege.

Unlike the art galleries of many other countries, the Rijksmuseum, the Stedelijk Museum and the Van Gogh Museum have concentrated on the works of their own great artists. These collections of masterpieces are not to be missed, although it is a sad reflection of our times that *The Night Watch*, housed in the Rijksmuseum, has to be shielded from damage by bullet-proof glass.

But then there have always been isolated groups eager to take advantage of Amsterdam's tradition of tolerance, be it today's sexual freedom, or the freedom of worship that made the city a safe haven for Protestants when most of Europe was beset by religious wars.

Amsterdam has, somehow, always found room for the oppressed, which is why, in the 17th century, secret Roman Catholic churches were created in the attics of houses; some were never unearthed by the Protestant zealots and survive to this day. There was a less happy ending in the Anne Frank House where the Jewish family hid from the Nazis until they were discovered, and where Anne scribbled down the diary that was eventually to catch the imagination of the world.

The main art galleries are open from Tuesday to Saturday, and on Sunday afternoon. The Amstelkring Museum, at 40 Voorburgwal, is open all day on Monday as well and is where you will find the best preserved of the clandestine Catholic churches, known as 'Onze Lieve Heer op Solder', 'Our Dear Lord in the Attic'. The Anne Frank House is at 263 Prinsengracht, open every day but especially crowded at weekends.

HOTEL Ambassade

This hotel on the Herengracht canal was created from a row of seven 17th-century houses, now knocked together but without ruining their original appearance. The public rooms and bedrooms are stuffed with antiques, the stairs are old, difficult and dangerous, but the atmosphere is marvellous. Bed and big breakfast only, but as the hotel is centrally situated this presents no problem.

Detail from The Night Watch

RHINE

The valley of the River Weser is the land of legends: of the Pied Piper of Hamelin, of Snow White and the Seven Dwarfs, and, a little further south, of the castle of the Sleeping Beauty and of the tower where Rapunzel, imprisoned by a witch, let down her golden hair so that her princely lover could scale the wall to spend the night with her.

It was also the home of the ultimate teller of tall tales, Baron von Münchhausen, who lived in the castle at Bodenwerder, when he was not travelling on imaginary adventures to the Russian steppes. His tallest tale was when he arrived at a town in the middle of winter, tied his horse to a pointed stake, and went to sleep. When he woke up, he found that the snow had melted and that his horse was tied to the top of the church steeple.

Other stories, however, do have some basis in fact. The citizens of Hamelin did have a dispute with an itinerant ratcatcher over his fee in 1284, after he had laid a trail of food to the river and disposed of most of the rats. On June 26 that year some of the children of Hamelin went out of the city to the nearby 'Poppenberg' Hill, and were never seen again. Whether there was any connection between the incidents, and whether the ratcatcher lured them away by playing his pipe, no one can say.

Many of the stories that have enchanted children for centuries might have been lost for ever but for the brothers Grimm, Jakob and Wilhelm, born 200 years ago, in Hanau. They were fascinated by folklore, and spent much

Baron von Münchhausen gets carried away

of their lives collecting fragments of stories which grew in the telling. In Kassel, on the Weser, between 1812 and 1815, they put together one of the world's most famous books, *Grimm's Fairy Tales*.

Between Hamelin and Kassel is the Solling-Vogler nature reserve, said to have been the home of the Seven Dwarfs who gave shelter to Snow White. The wicked Queen who several times tried, unsuccessfully, to have her beautiful stepdaughter removed for good, came from Alfeld, a pretty place on the nearby River Leine.

In the midst of another and larger forest, Reinhard, lies the Schloss Sababurg, which is, according to legend, where the Sleeping Beauty, a victim of the witch's curse, pricked her finger on a spinning wheel and fell into a sleep for one hundred years. It is easy to see how the story could have gained credence among the peasants, for the castle, built in the 14th century and surrounded by dense undergrowth, served mainly as a hunting lodge and was left unoccupied for long periods.

To the north-west, in yet more woodland, is the old university city of Marburg on the River Lahn, a cluster of narrow, medieval streets dominated by its 13th-century palace. This is where Hansel and Gretel, abandoned in the woods by their poverty-stricken parents, were caught by a witch but managed to dispose of her in her own cooking fire. They then returned home laden with treasure, carried back across the Lahn by an obliging white duck . . . or so the story goes.

The Lahn flows into the Rhine just south of Koblenz, where the great river is, perhaps, at its best, carving a deep rocky furrow down to Bingen, past another clutch of castles and vineyards which produce the famous Rhein Wein. Amongst the most striking of these castles are the Mouse Tower at the entrance to the Rhine Gorge; the Pfalz, standing on a rock in the middle of the river, where passing ships had to pay a toll to keep the castle cannon silent; and Reichenstein, with a robber baron who would have been a plausible character in the *Prisoner of Zenda*. The most famous landmark on the Rhine is, of course, the Lorelei rock, where legend has it that a beautiful woman sat combing her hair, distracting the sailors so that their ships were wrecked or grounded. The local prince tried to leap on to the rock to meet her, but fell short and was drowned. When his distraught father ordered the woman to be seized, she summoned white chargers by magic, and was carried into the Rhine.

There is a whole range of river trips on the Rhine, the upper Weser and the Neckar, although they are a means of sightseeing, not of quick travel: the journey from Heidelberg to Stuttgart, on one of the loveliest stretches of the Neckar, takes up to ten hours. However, the railway runs alongside the Rhine for long stretches, providing an attractive option for the return journey for motorists who need to recover their cars at the end of the day.

Heidelberg

Further south another tributary of the Rhine, the River Neckar, leads to Heidelberg, where the town, castle and forest backcloth rise in one magnificent setting. A cable railway takes you to the castle, a complete but charming ruin, and on up to Königstuhl, 2,000 feet above sea level. The view of the Neckar valley is superb, with the river flowing between the Black Forest and the Swabian Mountains.

Heidelberg University is the oldest in Germany. In earlier times the students, who often made a lasting career out of becoming educated, had their own inns and prisons – the first frequently leading to the second.

HOTEL Eisenhut

In the 14th century walled Bavarian town of Rothenburg ob der Tauber, on Germany's Romantic Road (see page 16), a hotel of great charm and character, created by knocking together four medieval houses. Luxurious, expensive, superb setting. Its fame, however, has made the Eisenhut too much in demand in high season.

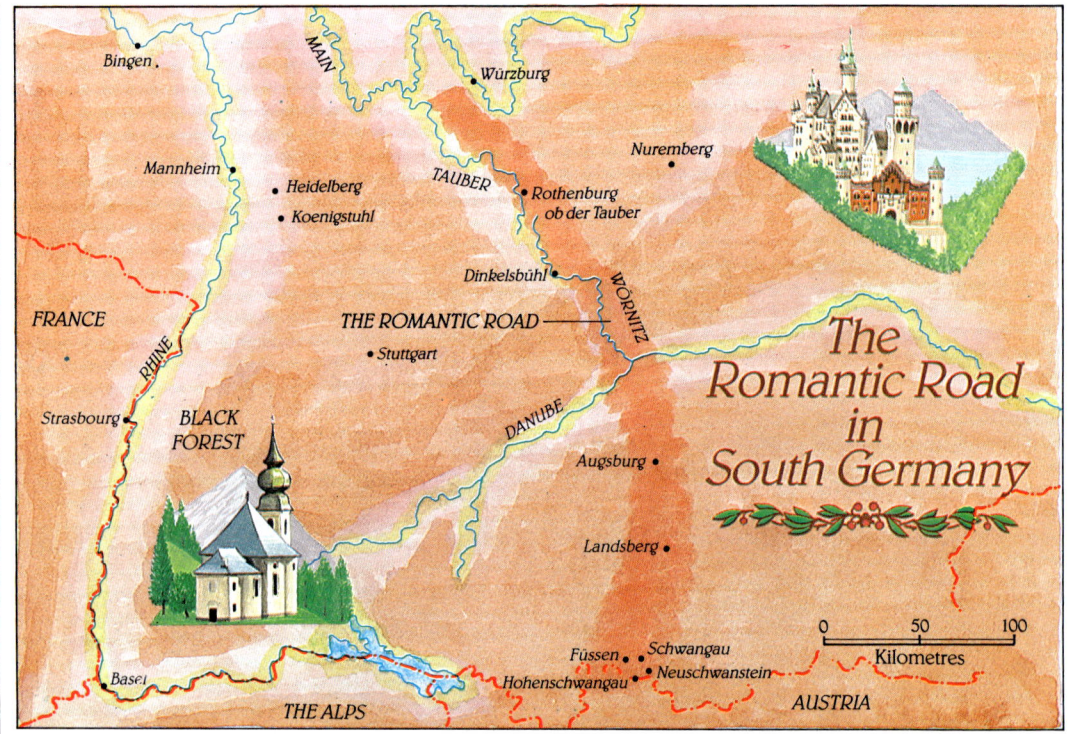

The Romantic Road

From Würzburg to the east, begins Germany's most celebrated route between the River Main and the Alps, trodden by travellers for centuries.

Rothenburg ob der Tauber was the legendary home of King Thrushbeard, the name given to him by a neighbouring king's rude daughter who rejected his suit, comparing his crooked chin to the beak of a thrush. Her furious father made her marry the first beggar who came along, a shabby minstrel who took her on a tour of King Thrushbeard's kingdom before revealing himself to be . . . the very same King Thrushbeard.

Part of his kingdom was the 800-year-old town of Dinkelsbühl, which has a perfectly preserved medieval market place. Surrounded by the Swedes, in 1632, during the Thirty Year's War, the town was saved from sacking by the Dinkelsbühl children, who went outside the walls to plead with their conquerors. Every year, during a festival that takes place during the third week in July, the local schoolchildren re-enact the event.

What history and legend could not provide was left to Ludwig II, the mad King of Bavaria, who reigned from 1864 to 1886. Where the Romantic Road climbs towards the Alps and the Austrian frontier, Ludwig built Neuschwanstein, whose resemblance to a fairy-tale castle can best be explained by the fact that the plans were drawn up by a painter of theatrical scenery. Hopelessly in debt, Ludwig was eventually dethroned by his indignant subjects.

Schlosshotel Lisl

For those who wish to savour the atmosphere whilst at dinner and breakfast, Schlosshotel Lisl at Schwangau has a unique view of two castles, Hohenschwangau, next door, and Ludwig's Neuschwanstein, both of which are floodlit for much of the year. The rooms are comfortable, the food excellent, and there is bathing in the hotel swimming pool and a nearby lake.

Neuschwanstein Castle

TIVOLI

As every schoolboy knows, Hadrian built a wall to keep out assorted hooligans, very few of whom were actually Picts and Scots. It says rather more for Italian culture, a good deal less for our own, that only four years later, in 125 AD, he ordered work to begin on a rather less military enterprise, the Villa Adriana, undoubtedly the most luxurious house ever built in ancient Rome.

Hadrian's Villa took nine years to complete, a reflection of the staggering demands it made on money and manpower. For this was no ordinary house: it was indeed the Versailles of the Roman Empire, capable, with its guest quarters, its swimming pools and its gymnasium, of accommodating and entertaining almost an entire army. Built on a hillside, it is adorned with sparkling fountains, huge marble statues, artificial lakes, grottoes, pools and rivers, and whole avenues of cypress trees.

Hadrian was not content to enjoy the best that Rome itself could offer. For a man whose journeys about the Roman Empire had been in the company of soldiers and in largely hostile country, he had found time to take in a great deal of his surroundings. The architects of his villa were bombarded with sketches, designs and even technical drawings by their enthusiastic Emperor, each some aspect of the classical world he had seen and admired. To describe them as replicas is to do them scant justice. Among the many marvels is the Canopus, a unique copy of the Egyptian City alongside the canal that led to the Temple of Serapis in ancient Canope, and the Pecile, a great four-sided gateway which is a perfect copy of the famous Stoa Poikile gate in Athens. The whole dwelling was linked by exquisite squares, including the d'Oro or Golden Square, with columns and porticoes in perfect symmetry. From all parts of the Empire and beyond, Hadrian brought statues and mosaics, paintings and furniture to embellish his creation.

The Villa Adriana became the favourite resort of the Emperors and was added to by Hadrian's successors, but the fall of the Roman Empire brought its eventual ruin. The Villa was sacked by the barbarians and the wrecked masonry was removed by enterprising peasants to build houses in nearby Tivoli. But many of Hadrian's treasures survived, to be discovered in excavations of the site, which began as early as the Renaissance, on the orders of the Popes. Even in ruin, Hadrian's Villa retains its majestic splendour and evocative atmosphere.

On the outskirts of Tivoli is the equally famous Villa d'Este, a Benedictine monastery which was transformed into one of the wonders of the world by Cardinal Ippolito d'Este. Although the villa has a beautiful 15th-century gateway, a Benedictine cloister, and a remarkable collection of paintings acquired by the Cardinal, it is the gardens which are truly superb. Walk from terrace to terrace, and you come upon a succession of exquisite cascading fountains. Behind lie cypress trees, each several hundred years old. The Organ Fountain derives its name from the ingenuity of a Frenchman, Claude Venard, who found a way to make the fountain drive a hydraulic organ and, thereby, create an astonishing combination of sound and

Fountain in the gardens of the Villa d'Este

water. The pièce de résistance is, however, the path lined with jets of water, the Avenue of the Hundred Fountains.

Tivoli itself is a town of considerable charm with many narrow medieval streets, perched on a hill of olive groves overlooking the Anio river, a tributary of the Tiber. It has been a spa since Roman times, and its waters are said to have healing properties, especially for rheumatism and skin diseases. There are four huge pools, together capable of accommodating no fewer than 5,000 bathers. The water, drawn from two nearby lakes, keeps to a precise depth and an exact temperature of 24 degrees throughout the year. The baths are linked to the main town by the Lucano Bridge, a strategic point which changed hands many times over the centuries. On the right bank nearby, human remains 30,000 years old have been discovered, as well as a cup with a wolf carving, suggesting that the legend of the founding of Rome by Romulus, a son of the gods brought up by a she-wolf, extended far beyond her walls.

Rome

A history of Black Market tickets would probably begin at the Colosseum, because there were never enough seats (though it held 50,000 spectators at a pinch) for the outstanding spectacles which, incidentally, were not Lions versus Christians but mock naval battles, for which the entire arena was flooded to the depth of several feet. Indeed, some of the re-enactments were said to be on a larger scale than the original battle, but then in Rome everything has always been larger than life, including the traffic, which, at best, is simply chaotic – a queue of shrilling snails in the rush hours – and, at worst, is positively malevolent, with drivers like frustrated charioteers. If you have a car, abandon it, at the first opportunity, locked in a locked garage. This will in no sense be a sacrifice, because the only way to see Rome is on foot. The city is a master of the surprise – at every corner some marvellous building or statue leaps out to be appreciated. It is also remarkably compact, with all its treasures

Ruins of Ancient Rome in a 17th-century engraving

within easy reach of one another. For the new visitor to Rome, not to be missed, apart from the Colosseum, are the Roman Forum, the Imperial Forum, the Palatine Hill and the Pantheon, while no one should leave Rome without at least one visit to St Peter's, the Vatican museums and the Sistine Chapel with its superb Michaelangelo ceiling.

The Villa Adriana is 14 miles east of Rome, six miles short of Tivoli itself. It is open from 9 am to one hour before sunset except on Mondays, and at Christmas, New Year, Easter, April 25, May 1, the first Sunday in June and August 15. It takes between 1½ and 2 hours to see the ruins of the Villa, which are scattered around the hillside. Anti-clockwise is by far the best route.

The Villa d'Este has similar opening times, but shuts slightly earlier, 1½ hours before sunset. It offers an exceptional *son et lumière* four nights a week between April and October.

A religious festival, the Inchinata, takes place on August 14 and 15 in Tivoli, with a spectacular procession.

For shopping in Rome: the Via Condotti at the foot of the Spanish Steps, where Gucci is by no means the most expensive establishment. For bargains: the flea market at Porto Portese every Saturday. For night life: the Trastavere district across the Tiber. For children: the Piazza Navona with its three fantastic fountains, sweet stalls and sometimes even Punch and Judy, Italian style.

Although the Rome authorities are making strenuous efforts to reduce street crime, with some success, handbags and wallets should be left behind, locked in the hotel safe. Rome is excessively crowded and hot in July and August, when the thieves are certainly not on holiday.

HOTEL Raphaël

Close to the Piazza Navona, with a wonderful roof garden where you can admire the Rome skyline at night – grandeur among the chimney pots. The hotel has an elegance which belies its modest prices, and air-conditioned rooms, strongly recommended in summer. Eat out.

POMPEII

On August 24, AD 79, the city of Pompeii ceased to exist. Around noon the nearby volcano, Vesuvius, finally forced an opening to the sky, hurling huge red hot boulders thousands of feet into the air, which rained down on Pompeii like thunderbolts from the gods. Some Roman historians claim that many of the citizens of Pompeii were enjoying entertainment in the amphitheatre when the blow struck, though there is no direct evidence of this. What is certain is that the rocks vomited by the mountain, and the shower of stone fragments that followed, almost demolished the city. Those citizens who escaped the bombardment and felt themselves spared, were suffocated by a deadly rain of ash which gave off sulphurous fumes. The ash not only destroyed the living: it preserved the dead in the midst of their everyday activities – a unique record of a Roman city by the sea.

Pompeii was an up-market resort, with a population of around 20,000, occasionally patronised by the Emperors. Its streets were extremely narrow, even by Roman standards, probably to provide some shade from the fierce Italian sun. The pavements, constructed from slabs of grey lava, were much higher than those of modern streets, and they needed to be. When Pompeii was not awash with water, much of it far from clean, its streets were piled high with rubbish, which is why huge stepping stones had to be placed across the street for the convenience of its citizens. You can still see the deep channels made between them by chariot wheels, and imagine the traffic jams which must have occurred at the crossroads amid much whip cracking and cursing.

But while Pompeii had its share of chaos and squalor, it also had some impressive public buildings: a huge basilica, the centre of law and commerce, opening out on to a rectangular forum; four luxurious public baths; and an amphitheatre which could seat almost the entire population. Undoubtedly their most popular entertainment was provided by the slave gladiators, some sixty of

Victim of Vesuvius

Stepping stones across one of Pompeii's roads

whom died helpless in their cells together with one luckless prostitute.

If there was anything the average citizen of Pompeii liked even more than brutal sport, then it was wild, uninhibited sex. Erotic wall-paintings and statues discovered in the ruins underline the extent of their obsession. When the eruption came, a good number of Pompeiians were trapped in the brothels, whose activities evidently continued to the last.

It was, of course, an age when early death through illness or violence was accepted as the norm, and people took their pleasures as they came. Pain was never far away, if the instruments found in the House of the Surgeon are anything to go by. He was evidently GP, obstetrician and dentist all rolled into one, with hideous pliers for extractions without anaesthetic, probes, catheters and knives for minor operations and amputations with the patient conscious (at any rate, at the start), and delivery forceps which would be enough to make any expectant mother faint right away.

Even in the grander houses, where life was lived to the full, there was a curious contrast between the magnificent and the disagreeable. Marvellous murals and mosaics tend to disguise the fact that most villas were entirely without windows. The houses had no proper heating, and yet in the public baths a complete heating system had been installed for the common citizen's use. Perhaps they were too busy electioneering, a passionate activity judging by the prolific writing of slogans on walls, urging the merits or shortcomings of this or that candidate. Graffiti like these are by no means the only problem to arise in the Roman Empire that has reappeared in modern times. In 59 AD a riot occurred in the amphitheatre at a sports meeting between the Pompeiians and Nucenians, which resulted in the theatre being shut for ten years. The Romans evidently believed in drastic remedies.

The volume of visitors to Pompeii is huge during the summer, when, to beat the coach parties, the independent traveller must arrive early in the morning. Even then, parking in Pompeii can present a serious problem. The easiest solution is to book a table at one of the nearby unashamedly tourist restaurants which has its own parking in the shade, and to complete your tour before the ravenous visitors arrive in droves at one o'clock. As the tourists in Pompeii are at their thickest around the Porto Marina entrance to the ruins and the Roman Forum, it makes sense to look at this part as early as possible, and aim to be far away, in the amphitheatre, when the main hordes arrive. One word of warning: Pompeii, perhaps wisely, has no stalls or snack bars inside the walls, so the demands of children for sustenance cannot be met at short notice. Also, the bumpy streets and high pavements mean that push chairs have to be lifted constantly.

Herculaneum

If Pompeii whets your appetite for the ruins of ancient Rome, Herculaneum, situated along the coast road south-east of Naples, offers an interesting contrast. Although Herculaneum was also destroyed by the eruption of 79 AD, it was not a victim of a molten bombardment or volcanic ash: rather, of the remorseless approach of a tide of mud flooding down from the slopes of Vesuvius. Consequently almost all of its inhabitants escaped, leaving a town preserved in petrified mud. Herculaneum was evidently a much quieter and more respectable place than Pompeii. Much more of the minutiae of life has been preserved, offering a unique view of the Romans in antiquity.

Capri

The complexity of local Italian politics means that the island has two mayors, one of whom would like to see more tourists visiting the island, the other who wants to ban them altogether. Well, not exactly. What he objects to are the day-trippers from Sorrento or Naples who spend as little money as pos-

Mosaic from Pompeii

sible and depart whence they came, leaving only their rubbish. Certainly at the height of the season, tourism reaches saturation point. The true beauty of Capri can be appreciated only at night, with its wonderful sunset and sunrise, with sun and later the moon reflected in a glorious blue crystal sea.

It is possible to escape the tourists in the daytime by hiring a boat and visiting the myriad of magical grottoes accessible only from the sea. The most famous, the Blue Grotto, is another tourist trap. To see it unspoilt, take a small boat with an outboard motor soon after dawn, when, incidentally, the light is at its best.

HOTEL Flora

Capri is still fashionable and still expensive, but the Flora offers perhaps the best value for money: a small pension near the main square, with many (though not all) of its 25 rooms offering a marvellous view of the sea. There is no restaurant, but with half a dozen within a few minutes walk, some people might find this a positive advantage.

Naples

Arguably the best panorama in Europe, the magnificent Bay of Naples with the slumbering (one hopes) volcano of Vesuvius behind the city. Naples also has the best slums, in the sense that their inhabitants seem in no way depressed by their poverty. For many, home is one room, so they eat their evening meal and watch TV in the narrow streets, and seem to enjoy the presence of passers-by. The other half of Naples eats, apparently with a clear conscience, in the luxurious fish restaurants of the harbour, where the food – and the bill – takes one's breath away.

HOTEL Royale

To have the stamina to enjoy Naples in hot weather, access to a swimming pool is more or less essential, and the Royale, on the waterfront (though a good walk from the quay with all the restaurants) is one of the few hotels to possess one . . . on the roof.

Amalfitan coast

In days gone by few travellers ventured on this rocky coast between Sorrento and Salerno. Perilous gorges spanned by uncertain bridges, jagged rocks that plunged directly to the sea, and medieval towers which were but a base for audacious pirates, combined to ensure that few survived the trip. The dangers have gone, but the wild beauty survives.

Vesuvius

For once an organised excursion is almost unavoidable, for while you can walk up the steep slope on the west side to the volcanic crater, from there on, it can be explored only in the company of a guide. The walk around the edge of the crater is not really dangerous if you act sensibly, although it would be unwise to take small children. The inside is something of an anti-climax: smouldering ashes rather than spouts of molten lava, except on those occasions when it would be prudent to be some distance away. The view, however, of the Campania countryside and the Bay of Naples, will linger in the mind's eye long after the holiday is a fleeting memory.

Vesuvius from Capri, across the Bay of Naples

SIENA

Siena is the most perfect surviving example of a medieval Italian city. Its Piazza del Campo, from which traffic is excluded, is the centre of Sienese life. Eleven streets lead into the square, which is shaped like a huge cockleshell, with the façades of medieval architecture providing a dramatic backcloth whichever direction you turn. On one side stands the Palazzo Pubblico, Siena's town hall, and one of the finest public buildings in Italy. The windows in its superb façade are adorned by the coats of arms of the city. The Palazzo has a brick tower, the Torre del Mangia, 286ft in height. The tower takes its name from a leading bellringer of the Middle Ages, when bellringing had a dual purpose: to summon the faithful to Mass, and to warn of imminent danger from fire within or the enemy without.

From the inner courtyard of the Palazzo you can climb to the top of the tower for a memorable view of the city. In particular, you can see its intricate pattern of gothic streets, its grand palaces and patricians' houses, monuments of an affluent age of city states when intrigue and artistic inspiration strode hand in hand.

In the Piazza del Duomo is the magnificent 13th-century cathedral, with unique paving which shows Biblical and allegorical scenes, the work of several brilliant artists. However, the stones are suffering from the ravages of tourism, and are now exposed only on rare occasions. The woodwork of the stalls, and the famous 13th-century pulpit, are further masterpieces not to be missed.

From the north aisle, is the entrance to the Piccolomini Library, an incredible collection of books gathered together in the 16th century, the height of Siena's prestige and power as an independent city state.

A short walk from the Cathedral is the Pinacoteca, a picture gallery with an extraordinary collection of Sienese paintings from the 13th to the 16th century by some of the greatest painters in Italy including Ambrogio and Duccio.

The Piazza del Campo, Siena

The Palio

Whilst Siena is not exactly off the beaten track, it takes a determined tourist to reach it from the more familiar centres of Rome, Florence or Pisa. For the Sienese, this has been a blessing in disguise, leaving their traditions largely untouched by the pursuit of the mark or the dollar.

One in particular, which began as an act of defiance against their Spanish overlords, is now the symbol of the spirit of Siena. Twice a year, on the feast days of the Madonna, the people of Siena run the Palio, the horse race to end all horse races, a step back in history.

For centuries Italy was simply a collection of city states, which fought little wars in a world where intrigue was a way of life. Even the cities were divided into districts or family groups, like the Montagues and the Capulets of Verona in *Romeo and Juliet*. In Siena, the districts, or contradas, dominate every aspect of life: to this day, if a man wishes to marry, sell his house, go into business, or decide where to educate his son, to do so without consulting the elected elders of the contrada would be unthinkable. The children of the contradas are said to be baptised twice, once in church soon after birth, and again by the contrada's chosen priest within the confines of its district.

There are seventeen contradas with picturesque, evocative names, reflecting past

The Palio

tasks, triumphs and failures. Citizens of Siena belong to the Unicorn, the Dragon, the She-Wolf, the Eagle, the Panther, the Ram, the Giraffe, the Goose, the Porcupine, the Tortoise, the Caterpillar, the Snail, the Owl, the Shell, the Forest, the Wave or the Tower. Each has its own vivid colours and costumes, which at the time of the Palio are displayed in a great parade around the Campo. Before the race comes the battle of the banners, a contest to see which of the flag bearers can hurl his flag the highest without the ignominy of allowing it to fall to the ground. As the banner unfurls, it seems almost alive, requiring stupendous skill to keep it in play.

All the horses come from Tuscan farriers and are chosen strictly by lot. They may have to race in as many as six trials before the Palio itself, and if one of the final ten is injured it cannot be replaced. Its contrada will take part in the parade with furled banner and muffled drums, with the hoofs of its horse carried with due ceremony on a black cushion. Casualties are all too common on the sandy track laid on top of the Campo's paving stones, and the tight corners often cause a horse to crash into one of the surrounding walls.

The trials are as much a test for the jockey as for the horse, because riders can be changed, and frequently are, before the Palio itself. Jockey is a derogatory term in Siena for someone who cannot be trusted, and these jockeys have added a fresh dimension to the concept of double-dealing. Many are herdsmen from the Roman plains east of the Tiber, and this is a rare opportunity for them to make real money. They strike bargains with rival contradas and rival jockeys in a merry-go-round of intrigue and counter-intrigue.

If that were not enough to cause a shudder among the Stewards at Newmarket, the start, called the mossa, is truly chaotic. The starter, often disguised, rather like a headsman of old, to shield his true identity (for passions run high at the Palio), draws the order by lot and then has the formidable task of lining up nine horses behind a rope without starting gates. The tenth horse, reckoned to be at a huge disadvantage on the outside, is allowed a flying start from behind a second rope. Small wonder that there are many false starts – thirteen in all in 1983, when the Palio had to be postponed until the following day.

The race itself is a mad dash of uninterrupted violence. The jockeys ride bareback, and wield riding crops on opponents and mounts with no apparent discrimination. There are bone-jarring collisions on corners, riders are thrown off and trampled, to be rescued at considerable personal risk.

After three circuits of the track, the winning contrada receives the Palio itself, a tall banner painted with the shields of the victors. It will be displayed in all its glory at the street banquet held in the successful district, a trestle-tabled triumph of epic proportions that lasts deep into the night.

If any further evidence was needed to demonstrate that the Palio is no ordinary horse race, then it must be the fact that a riderless mount is permitted to win, and has done on several occasions down the years. This rule was introduced when one contrada, more ruthless than the rest (if that were possible), employed an assassin with a crossbow to shoot a rival jockey off his horse a few yards from the finish. The Palio is indeed a matter of life and death.

The Palio takes place on July 2 and August 16. Tiered seats are placed around the Piazza del Campo. A place can be purchased . . . at a price; there is a flourishing black market.

HOTEL Park

On a hill some three miles from Siena, with a winding access road that is difficult to find and has a hairpin bend that will cause most cars to do a three-point turn, the Park sits in splendid isolation. An old Tuscan villa, restored with considerable taste and style by the Ciga group, it offers luxurious accommodation, exceptional food, and wonderful views of the Italian countryside. Tired tourists, back from a hard day's sightseeing in the city, can soak away the dust beside, and within, the swimming pool.

——— INTERLAKEN ———

Interlaken, the town 'between the lakes', is overlooked by towering mountain ranges, with turbulent air currents and deceptive mists. This ensures that visitors whose lives back home are lived more or less on the end of a runway, can find true contentment, for there is no airport and, while this resort in the very heart of Switzerland can be easily reached by road, in truth the train is king.

Built on a plateau 1,770 feet above sea level between the lakes of Thun and Brienz, Interlaken was first appreciated by the Victorians, who tried all too successfully to turn it into something it was not: a kind of Bognor-on-the-Lake, complete with tree-lined boulevards, immaculate promenades and ornate hotels.

Without the British influence, however, Interlaken might never have achieved its link with a network of mountain railways, whose motivation was tourism from the very beginning. For if skiing other than as a means of transport existed in a small way in late Victorian times, though rather more obviously in Norway than in Switzerland, the visitors of those days liked to take their pleasures with a modicum of comfort.

The Jungfrau 13,642ft

This excursion depends entirely on the weather for its success. If you cannot see the tops of the mountains from Interlaken, the logic is irrefutable: you will not be able to see anything from the top either, so do not waste time and money trying. Clear days are extremely rare outside the summer months. If crocodiles of Japanese tourists arrive with the obvious intention of going to the top, it does not mean that they have some miraculous insight into an imminent change in the weather: simply that they have bought their tickets months in advance.

The starting point is the railway station at Interlaken Ost, the ideal place to park if you have arrived at Interlaken by car. From here you join the BOB – not a bobsleigh but Bernese Oberland Railways, whose friction/

Jungfrau railway

rack service to Lauterbrunnen, at a mere 2,612 feet, began in 1890. At Wilderswil, on its route, you may catch a glimpse of BOB's next prodigious feat, the pure rack railway up to Schynige Platte with 1 in 4 gradients and, at peak times, the rather forbidding sight of trains following each other at a distance of one hundred yards. But as the red and white railway pulls out of sight, the sense of loss is only temporary: you take a similar train yourself on the way down. For the present, the only way is up. At Lauterbrunnen, change to the green train of the Wengernalp Railway, opened in 1893. The longest single stretch of rack railway in Switzerland, its twists and turns are truly fantastic, on viaducts, over bridges and through tunnels with the clicks of the cogwheels outmatched by the clicks of the tourists' cameras. Sheer waterfalls, valleys with near perpendicular, yet still tree-clad, sides, and the great mountain peaks, offer breathtaking scenes which succeed one another almost too quickly for the mind to assimilate – and there is still more to come.

At Kleine Scheidegg, all of 6,762 feet above the sea, sits the station where the Wengernalp Railway ends and passengers must change platforms for the brown and cream livery of the ultimate mountain railway, the Jungfrau. Hikers and skiiers are soon left far below as the rack railway climbs 4,500 feet in a mere six miles of track. This is no modern marvel, as the four sections were constructed between 1896 and 1912, an astonishing engineering achievement. On the first section, to Eigergletscher, at 7,612 feet, the train offers stunning views of the Jungfrau, the Mönch, and the treacherous north face of the Eiger, which the track proceeds to climb . . . but on the inside. Just beyond Eigergletscher Station, the train plunges into a tunnel, 4.5 miles long, which seems to defy many of the laws of nature. Twice the train stops, first at Eigerwand, 9,400 feet, when all but the very summit of the Eiger is now below, and then at Eismeer, in amongst the snows at 10,368 feet. At each station, huge windows have been cut out of the mountainside to provide an unforgettable panorama.

The train climbs higher, sometimes on 1 in 4 gradients, passing through the heart of the Mönch mountain, until it reaches Jungfrau, the highest railway station in Europe. The station is still underground, but an elevator takes the passengers up to the 11,720ft high Sphinx terrace. From here, a glacier ten miles long stretches into the beyond. Once satiated by the view, visitors can see the ice palace, have a skiing lesson, send a postcard home from Europe's highest post office, or eat in the highest restaurant. The meal is scarcely for the gourmet, but they probably have problems with the help.

On the way down, the skyline is dominated by the north face of the Eiger, still one of the severest tests for mountaineers, but mastered by machinery. The Jungfrau Railway, practically never closed by the weather, is truly one of the wonders of the world.

Each summer Interlaken offers a series of performances in the open air (but with a covered and heated auditorium for the more delicate visitors) of the famous play 'William Tell' by the German dramatist, Johann Schiller. With a huge cast, and a good deal of action, it tells the story of the Swiss hero who is said to have confounded the Austrian governor, Gessler, by shooting an apple off his own son's head with a crossbow bolt. What *is* fact is that the Swiss Confederation ended the domination of the Austrian Hapsburgs by force of arms in the fourteenth century. Was William Tell, the legendary master of the mountain ambush, the catalyst, or a will-of-the-wisp, invented by one side to inspire victory or by the other to excuse defeat?

HOTEL Feischerblick

For those visitors not satiated by the ride to the Jungfrau, the Oberland Railway has an alternative loop through Grindelwald, which at a mere 3,393 feet, still provides awe-inspiring views of the peaks above. Where better to stay than on the main street of Grindelwald in this old chalet hotel, all wood panels and genuine antiques, and, providing you can manage the stairs, some lovely rooms with a superb outlook.

Serious mountaineers use it for rest rather than recreation: the rest of us can watch them at work from the agreeable terrace below. The Feischerblick closes in May, November, the first half of December and the second half of April.

BRUGES

When medieval Europe was a place of pillage and destruction, Bruges offered stability and prosperity. From the 12th to the 16th century it was the largest trading centre in northern Europe, with a population close on 200,000, a prodigious statistic in days when kingdoms stretched barely as far as the eye could see and armies were tiny.

It was one such army which took part in the Second Crusade of 1147, a military exercise so staggeringly inept that the forces of the Emperor Conrad III and King Louis VII of France took entirely different routes to the Holy Land, fought separately, and succeeded only in discrediting the entire movement. In such a dismal context one man, Derreck of Alsace, Count of Flanders, acquitted himself with such bravery that he was presented with the Relic of the Holy Blood by the Patriarch of Jerusalem. It consisted of a tiny crystal phial, sealed with a golden stopper hung on silver chains, said to contain a few drops of the blood-stained water remaining after the body of Christ had been washed in preparation for burial by Joseph of Arimathea. The relic was carefully guarded by the followers of Jesus, and handed down from father to son, so it must have been a remarkable feat of courage by Derreck to merit such recognition. Curiously, the Count did not return himself with the relic to Flanders, but entrusted it to his chaplain. If its long journey from the Holy Land proved uneventful, the relic thereafter had a charmed life. It was sought, unsuccessfully, by the Calvinists and later by the French Revolutionaries, and was hidden in cellars and rafters by citizens of Bruges at the risk of their lives. Earlier, when Bruges was attacked by Ghent in a 14th-century quarrel, some soldiers threw the phial into the river and it was thought lost for ever. But three days later, one of the sisters from the beguinage, home of the widows of Crusaders, saw the phial reflecting the glare of the sun just beneath the water, and rescued it in triumph. In an age of religious fervour, this was indeed a miracle.

The relic, now restored to its place of prominence in the religious life of Bruges, rests behind the tabernacle of the altar in the Chapel of the Holy Blood. Each year, on Ascension Day, it is carried triumphantly in procession through the streets, an occasion of great passion and pageantry. The procession, which is preceded by a mass at St Saviour's Cathedral, had its origins in the oath of allegiance sworn by the burghers of Bruges to their feudal lords. They risked eternal damnation, or any rate thought they did, if they broke a promise made while touching the relic, which was then shown to the watching crowds for further effect. This custom was gradually transformed into a procession around the ramparts of the city, and whilst not all the ramparts have survived, the procession is held every year.

It is a brilliant, animated occasion, begun by young girls in flowing, deep blue cloaks, singing the 'Veni Creator'. They are followed by spectacular and sometimes moving portrayals of episodes from the Bible, beginning with the calling of Abraham, eventually leading to the Crucifixion and the missions of the Apostles. It is a mixture of mime, speech and song, in colourful tableaux which, in earlier days, offered an opportunity for the merchants of Bruges to outdo one another in munificence. Yet the simplest scene is the most evocative, an actor, as Christ, carrying a huge wooden cross, and stumbling beneath its weight.

The mood, at once stunning and sombre, changes with the enactment of the entry of Derreck, Count of Flanders, into Bruges. Ignoring the historical niceties, he is accompanied by an exquisite golden shrine containing the phial of Holy Blood, borne aloft by the bishops and their clergy. Bannered trumpets announce their arrival; first come foot soldiers in fawn belted tunics over vivid red livery, followed by the mounted horse of the Count and his Lady, armoured menace in the cause of Christ. After an hour of breathtaking spectacle, the participants mingle together again in the Burg Square, ranks of Roman soldiers with bronze shields and gleaming spears coming face to face with medieval cavalry, as though time had played a bizarre trick on the senses.

A day later, Bruges will be back to normal, a city in which the motor car is grudgingly permitted as a 20th century intruder into a society that hankers after its past. When, or perhaps if, you find a place to park, you soon forget how you came, and are ecstatically stifled by the all-pervading atmosphere of calm and contentment. Narrow cobbled streets, with tiny gabled houses and neat little bridges over deceptively motionless canals, lead in their turn to an apparent suspension of time at the beguinage, an oasis of tranquillity. Once over the humpbacked bridge and beneath the curious arched gateway, you feel constrained to hold your breath indefinitely for fear of imposing on the serenity of its silence.

Although Bruges is worth a major detour on any day of the year – it is at its best on a Sunday, when the suspension of modern commerce adds to its prodigious appeal – visitors who hope to watch the Procession of the Holy Blood must plan ahead. Reservations for the stands and benches at vantage points are taken by the Tourist Office from the previous February, although some tour companies anticipate the problem of tickets for their clients by block booking in advance. Belgian Railways, with a nice sense of occasion and perhaps an eye for business, offer a 50 per cent reduction from most stations on procession day.

HOTEL Duc de Bourgogne

Its diners, in a candlelit restaurant which leans spectacularly over the water at the meeting of two canals, are the envy of passers-by, kept at respectful distance on the nearest bridge. Banks of vivid flowers lead the eye to the distant sight of Bruges' towered skyline, interrupted only by the serving of another stupendous course. Nothing seems to disconcert the staff, be it baby-sitting for baby or coping with guests determined to leave during the night. With only nine rooms, immaculately furnished, most with breathtaking views, the Duc de Bourgogne offers a memorable experience – but do not expect it to be cheap.

PASSING PARIS

Barbizon

Lying in the heart of lush green countryside but still less than an hour's drive from Paris, Barbizon was adopted by the great French painters, Jean François Millet and Theodore Rousseau. If the main street of this tiny village has become tastefully commercial, with restaurants and antique shops jostling for space, and double yellow lines waging war on the motorist, the ambience is untouched and the scenery striking. You can see the house where Millet lived, when he was not put up for nothing at the Père Ganne Inn.

HOTEL Le Bas-Breau

If money is no object, Le Bas-Breau is an outstanding hotel with beautiful rooms and memorable food – as memorable as the final bill. Robert Louis Stevenson stayed here (but he must have got a discount); Mrs Thatcher also went there for the Fontainebleau conference in 1983.

Vaux-le-Vicomte

A visit from Louis XIV was always a hazardous affair. Louis' Minister of Finance, Nicolas Fouquet, discovered this for himself. In a corrupt age, in which men of power and influence were showered with gifts in the hope that the favour might one day be returned, Fouquet was notorious for his lack of scruples. Between 1657 and 1661 Fouquet misappropriated funds from the French treasury on a mind-boggling scale to build the Château of Vaux-le-Vicomte, a fabulous moated castle in a matchless, landscaped setting. When the Château was virtually complete, Fouquet entertained the king to a magnificent banquet, which quite outshone anything at the royal court. Louis thanked his host and departed, but three weeks later Fouquet was arrested. His wealth and his Château were seized by the king, along with the creators of its splendour, the architect Le Vau, the interior designer Le Brun and the landscape gardener Le Nôtre. They were set a

Château of Vaux-le-Vicomte

new task, to build a palace for the king that would eclipse every building in France, and they achieved it – at Versailles.

Vaux-le-Vicomte, unusually for its size, is privately owned, bought by a millionaire sugar manufacturer a century ago, whose grand-daughter married a French count. It therefore charges visitors rather more than châteaux run by the state, but the cost of its upkeep must be enormous.

Chantilly

They close the Château of Chantilly on race days, presumably on the grounds that the nearby racecourse could attract the undesirable visitor, who might extend his revelry or his recriminations among its sumptuous furnishings. The Château, built on two small islands in the middle of a small lake, is easily the most remarkable to be found outside the valley of the Loire. Inside, is an unsurpassed collection of early illuminated manuscripts; outside, a sylvan park created with a total disregard for expense. The owners, the Condé family, devoted most of their energy to a different passion. They hunted almost literally from dusk to dawn, reducing grooms, horses and dogs to near exhaustion in pursuit of their pleasure. This is why the present-day stables at Chantilly are dwarfed by the magnificent 18th-century stables, which accommodated 240 horses and 500 hounds.

The Condé family were cousins of Louis XIV, who, in April, 1671, invited himself to stay. His arrival at Chantilly, together with several hundred courtiers, was a deliberate challenge to the great chef, Vatel, who had refused a post at Court. Vatel ransacked the countryside for supplies but the task of feeding no fewer than 4,800 guests proved too much. His first dinner of roast meats was inadequate, and two tables went without a main course. The next day, when the fish that was due to provide his *pièce de résistance* failed to arrive, Vatel retired to his chamber and killed himself. He was a little premature, as the fish turned up a few minutes later.

Chartres

The Cathedral of Chartres, with its pale gold towers dominating the skyline for miles, is truly one of the wonders of France. It had barely been completed in 1194 when most of it was destroyed in a disastrous fire; but the townspeople were inspired by the dramatic rescue of what was said to be the veil of the Virgin Mary, worn by her at the birth of Christ, to rebuild it. The veil is still preserved in the Chapel of St Piat. During the rebuilding, which took almost 30 years, the masterpieces of sculpture were added to the walls. But what makes Chartres worth a journey in itself are the 13th-century stained glass windows, marvellous shades of blue, which run through a remarkable sequence of changes according to the light. The city council made the courageous decision to have the windows dismantled during both the First and the Second World War, more than 3,000 square feet of separate pieces, an awe-inspiring task. Their survival intact has been its own reward.

Although the Cathedral *is* Chartres, its old houses and narrow streets, especially along the river Eure, are delightfully picturesque. Walking is the only practical way to see Chartres, which is well served with car parks, although owners of long or large cars should be warned that the spiral ramps in the underground park are extremely tight and many vehicles almost need to be shoe-horned into a space.

HOTEL Le Grand Monarque

An old coaching inn, dating back to the days when Chartres was two days journey from Paris, now an elegant hotel close to the cathedral. Its food, once the best to be found in the city, is now erratic. All the rooms have private facilities, many with antique porcelain, but with equally antique plumbing. When booking, which is essential in high season, stipulate a room overlooking the quiet courtyard at the back.

North Rose window of Chartres Cathedral

CANNES

The Film Festival

The Cannes Festival is always in danger of becoming a parody of itself: a liberal sprinkling of film stars, whose only fear is that someone will fail to recognise them; a posse of starlets, whose efforts to be trapped on celluloid for ever have been frustrated by the increasingly liberal attitude to life (although full marks for trying to the naked lady who arrived for lunch on the sea front by helicopter); and those other essential ingredients of the Festival, the jury, the press photographers, the bodyguards, the hangers-on and the gatecrashers. Oh, and I almost forgot, the public.

In Festival week each May, Cannes is a poseur's paradise. Simply by loafing nonchalantly on the steps of the Convention centre, it is almost impossible not to be photographed with someone who is someone. If you are unscrupulous, ingenious and naturally gregarious, you may also find yourself inside the security cordon of one of the scores of parties held during the week, for which a pre-

requisite is speaking English, preferably with a slight accent, looking well dressed, and almost knowing someone who actually does know someone.

If you disapprove of gatecrashing on moral grounds, it may still become a necessity for financial reasons. For Cannes, always expensive, is breathtakingly so during this premier week, especially at the hotels and restaurants on the tree-lined Boulevard de la Croisette, which is a cross between Brighton sea front and the Monaco Grand Prix, except that the Grand Prix only lasts a couple of hours. It is difficult to convey the level of potential expenditure, but it is noticeable how the staff at reception in some of the most luxurious hotels perceptibly sneer at anything less than a gold credit card and put you in a room at the back.

That is, always assuming they give you a room at all, because the normal rules of confirmed bookings are suspended during the festival. Overbooked guests are swopped like spies by rival hotels which would not be seen dead acknowledging one another's existence the rest of the year. If you cannot see the sea

A private beach at Cannes

from your hotel room, at least you can cross the incredibly dangerous main road and sit on the beach . . . at a price. Most of the beaches, certainly all those remotely near the Film Festival, are owned by the same luxurious hotels which charge for the use of a deck chair, a sun umbrella, an air mattress (almost as much as buying one, but just try bringing your own) and an enormous sum for a mediocre lunch.

Now that film budgets have gone the way of all flesh and are noticeably sagging, hiring a yacht is a means of saving money as an alternative to a hotel, rather than a supplementary means of giving a thrash. You can tell which companies are trying to save money: their yachts will be moored at the obscure back end of the harbour, a taxi ride along the Croisette and, even then, it's like looking for a needle in a haystack. Once arrived, the biggest problem for gatecrashers is distinguishing between the crew members pretending to be owners and the owners themselves. Either way, apart from a token trip around the bay, very few of them ever actually put to sea.

The success of the Festival depends on two factors: the weather, and who wins. The weather is easier to predict, because it is nearly always sunny, though rarely warm enough to swim. Although the era when a whole circus was hired to publicise the United States entry, *Around the World in 80 Days*, has disappeared never to return, American money is still essential to keep the Festival going, so they have to win, if not every year, then nearly every year. To quote a gentleman of the jury: 'Sure we have a free hand, like Dubchek had a free hand when the Russians took him in chains to Moscow.' Sometimes they rebel, and pick the best film for the hell of it.

The Festival owes its existence indirectly to the former Lord Chancellor of England, Lord Brougham, who abandoned plans to travel on to Nice in 1834 because of a cholera epidemic and stayed in Cannes, then a tiny fishing village. Lord Brougham liked it so much he came every winter for 34 years. He would not like it now.

HOTEL Colombe d'Or

Not actually in Cannes, but about 25 minutes by car, first along the autoroute towards Nice and then by a sinuous mountain road up to the Gorges du Loup to the ancient fortified town of St-Paul, built on a rocky spur. The hotel is easily missed because it looks discouragingly more like a house, with an entrance through a heavy wooden door into a stone courtyard. Only the presence of a dozen tables set for lunch or dinner convinces you that you are not trespassing on private property. If the food does not always match this magnificent setting, the ambience is quite marvellous, a world away from bustling Cannes and with incredible views of the Loup Valley. On each floor, reached by a stone staircase, as it would be almost impossible to install a lift, is a little antichamber where you can sit and recover your breath and take in the scenery.

Around Cannes

If you grow tired of the Boulevard de la Croisette, Cannes is the starting point of an outstanding tour of the Esterel Massif to the south-west. The twisting roads to St Raphaël offer breathtaking views of the coastline where the jagged volcanic rocks of the Esterel cut deep into the sea, fiery red crags contrasting vividly with deep blue bays. The roads were once a haven for bandits, who preyed on the travellers to Italy.

Beyond St Raphaël lies the surrealistic marina of Port Grimaud, with rows of canals and tiny humpbacked bridges, ingeniously designed to resemble an old French fishing village. Most of the houses have claustrophobic little gardens backing on to moorings, for this is where the yachting fraternity return home for dinner. You can take an excursion across the bay to St Tropez, whose fame as the home of Brigitte Bardot – her villa lies on an exclusive peninsula close by – is no longer quite so often backed up by ostentatious wealth in the shape of floating gin palaces in the main harbour.

To the east lies the Riviera proper, a cluster of beautiful harbours and beaches, the mecca of the rich and the envious every summer. Juan-les-Pins has a magnificent bay and gently sloping beach, sheltered by Cap d'Antibes, where only the staggeringly rich can afford a private villa.

Just before the Italian border lies Monaco, an independent principality (independent, that is, unless you go there in an attempt to evade French taxes). Its huge harbour, full of mind-boggling yachts, is overlooked by the Palace, where every day Inspector Clouseau turns up, in unfamiliar guise as a Monagasque lieutenant, to oversee the changing of the guard, an unforgettable shambles. Down in Monte Carlo itself is the Casino, whose public gaming rooms are a sad disappointment, full of scruffy slot machine addicts. The real gambling takes place in the Salons Privés late at night, where you can see the world's best-dressed bankrupts.

Closer to Cannes, deep in the hills, is the delightful town of Grasse, itself once an independent republic, and later a favourite of Queen Victoria, who wintered in the Grand Hotel. The streets of the old quarter, narrow and twisting with formidable ramps and steps, hide little restaurants whose food usually matches the ingenuity of their siting; presumably the chefs do not suffer from claustrophobia.

The prosperity of modern Grasse depends on its perfume industry. You cannot, as is popularly supposed, tour an actual factory; but you can visit a demonstration works, of which the most convenient is Fragonard, in the centre of the town with its own car park. Their shop offers factory prices, a real bargain, and accepts sterling.

Between Grasse and Cannes is the perched village of Mougins, once fortified and independent, with a 15th-century gateway, the only surviving entrance to the original ramparts. Its winding streets, where the houses on either side almost touch one another on the first or second floor, lead out into a little square full of delightful restaurants. This is the smart place to eat at night if you live or stay in Cannes. Cars are banned from the centre and the regulations are ruthlessly enforced by a formidable female Z-cars team on buzz bikes.

CARCASSONNE

Carcassonne was the largest fortress in Europe, but never an impregnable one, because its water supply was inadequate to sustain the number of defenders needed to man its walls. Its fall in 1209 after a siege of barely a month was a critical factor in one of the great religious wars, when a region of southern France was drenched in blood and one of the most advanced cultures in Europe totally exterminated.

This was the Albigensian crusade, the first against Christians, if Christians they were, because the Pope, Innocent III, declared them to be heretics. The Albigensians, named after the town of Albi near Toulouse, a bastion of their beliefs, believed that there were two co-eternal principals, one good and one evil, and that the material world was evil. They rejected most, if not all, of the Old Testament and regarded the Incarnation as an illusion. Salvation could be achieved by subduing earthly desires, so devout followers took vows of chastity and were vegetarians. These doctrines meant that the Roman Catholic Church had no role to play in religious salvation, and one of the main weapons of the Church, the fear of the masses that they might not qualify for a heavenly after-life, was totally lost. The sect gathered momentum when nobles in south-west France saw the new beliefs as an excuse to seize Church lands, for a Church without a function did not need territory and property. It was little wonder that the Pope took the desperate measure of launching a special crusade to end such heresy.

The crusade soon came to be led by Simon de Montfort, father of the Simon de Montfort who introduced into England an embryonic Parliament. De Montfort senior was no Parliamentarian, but a sadistic small town noble from the outskirts of Paris. The Pope gave him Carcassonne after the siege and its inhabitants had to endure his brutal rule until, as the Crusade continued, de Montfort was killed in a battle outside Toulouse.

The fortifications destroyed during the

Carcassonne

Albigensian wars were rebuilt by Philip III of France and, thereafter, Carcassonne became the symbol of royal power in south-west France, resisting the Black Prince and, later, the Huguenots during the Wars of Religion. However, its importance declined as siege weapons advanced, and the walls became a quarry in the 17th century, the local inhabitants taking away the stonework to build their own houses.

Carcassonne's fortifications might well have become simply a heap of rubble, had not the 19th-century architect, Viollet le Duc, answered an appeal from some archaeologists and visited the city. He was amazed by the potential of what he saw – 'I do not think there exists in Europe such a formidable set of defence works' he wrote in his diary – and he agreed to carry out the task of restoration. It was an epic undertaking, because Carcassonne had 52 towers with two concentric walls of defences and an outer circumference of almost two miles. Le Duc began rebuilding around 1845, but sadly did not live to see the full fruition of his work, which continued for

some years after his death. The result may have a few historical errors, and the fortifications are almost too perfect, a kind of medieval Disneyworld, but the skyline is truly stunning. The city, set on its hill, dominates the surrounding countryside, with the River Aude winding past below. All in all, worth a major journey to see it.

Carcassonne, now on a major motorway, the Autoroute des Deux Mers, receives a huge volume of visitors in the summer and parking outside the medieval city is more or less compulsory. Long queues can therefore be expected for the organised tour, which starts from the Countal Castle.

HOTEL Domaine d'Auriac

Not in Carcassonne itself, but a few miles to the south on route St Hilaire, in the centre of wooded grounds with a splendid terrace and swimming pool. At first glance it looks like an elegant private house; the rooms are extremely comfortable. The quality of the food is, however, variable.

———— MARBELLA ————

Marbella is made by its climate rather than its residents. Rain here is an event, winters are mild, and the hot summers are made more agreeable by a cooling wind blowing in from the sea. Nestling at the back of a bay fringed by blue-tinged mountains which merge with the sky, Marbella was never simply a fishing village like Benidorm or Lloret de Mar, transformed by tourism in an irreversible way. It had large private houses in secluded grounds long before package tourism was ever thought of, and has continued to keep one step ahead of mass travel. The aristocratic and the rich keep their distance from the all-inclusive holidaymaker by the simple expedients of moving either out of town, or out to sea.

The local authorities have now banned buildings of more than four storeys, making the high-rise hotels of Torremolinos impossible to emulate – if that is the correct word. Instead, property developers have been forced to use their imagination. They have built what are, in effect, hotels which spread outwards rather than upwards and are called clubs, although the only qualification for membership is that you can afford to stay and use the amenities. One such example is the Marbella Hill Club behind the town, which spreads itself over some 50 acres, with apartments and houses used by their owners a few weeks a year, and rented the rest.

The oldest, and the most famous, is the Marbella Club, now owned by an Arab property group but still run by the man, Prince Alfonso von Hohenlohe, who literally built it. The Prince, who was far from rich when he came to Marbella in the late 1950s, did not possess the wherewithal to bring in proper local contractors. He did his own hiring and led by example, laying bricks and mixing cement. What he lacked in resources he possessed in contacts, and the Marbella Club, right next to its own private beach, soon became as chic as the French Riviera.

In the '60s and '70s, moving to Marbella was not only a matter of fashion. Prices had risen enormously in the South of France, while in southern Spain, lavish accommodation and lavish meals, and enormous numbers of staff, could be acquired for a fraction of the cost. Not all the beautiful people were oblivious to value for money.

Marbella is now in the grip of a new phenomenon: a select group of visitors for whom money is, literally, no object. Along the 'Golden Mile', the most exclusive avenue by the beach, multi-millionaires have bought or built properties which they may use once or twice a year, but which remain empty, empty, that is, apart from their huge staff of butlers, maids, gardeners and chauffeurs. This is where the Kashoggis, Sheik Yamani and other oil moguls, and King Fahd of Saudi Arabia have their little places by the sea.

Such properties have minders that make Terry McCann look like a tame pussy cat, so holidaymakers will be ill-advised to attempt a stroll in the grounds to see how the other half really lives. They will have to be content with the occasional glimpse when the rich and famous go out to eat the superb seafood on offer at such smart and outrageously expensive restaurants as La Fonda, arguably one of the most attractive in Europe, the Meridiana, or La Hacienda, where the doorman probably drives more Rolls Royces than the man who tests them in Derby.

For a closer view of the trappings of the wealthy, the port of Puerto Banus offers the most expensive collection of aquatic real estate in the world, row upon row of yachts where the starting price would be in millions, ostentatious luxury at its splendid worst. The port, five miles from Marbella, will not be found on any antiquarian maps: it was created from nothing by José Banus, using a Swiss architect for the shops and houses, and a French designer to construct the marina.

Only one significant addition has been made to Puerto Banus since it was built, a jetty added specially to accommodate the truly stupendous yacht belonging to Adnan Kashoggi, worth, some say with only slight

Puerto Banus

exaggeration, more than all the other big boats in the harbour put together. Adnan Kashoggi has a habit of dropping in unexpectedly, which may help to explain why his personal jetty is decorated by a red carpet left permanently, if not altogether elegantly, in position, While the Kashoggi yacht is frequently to be seen on serious voyages, or at any rate elsewhere in the Mediterranean, this is the exception rather than the rule. Many of the big yachts here are effectively floating hotels, with skippers who have forgotten when they were last asked to hoist the anchor. Although the African coast is less than 50 miles away, the yacht owners would probably be quite horrified if any of their guests seriously suggested sailing there.

Puerto Banus, with 25 smart restaurants and twice that number of expensive boutiques, is a poseur's paradise, the ultimate pick-up point for anyone with access to a boat, or, for the less choosy, anyone with a scooter. It has a rather incongruous mixture of the extremely rich and the relatively poor, tourists alike, watching one another watch one another. Only the British expatriates keep away. They came to Marbella and its surroundings when it was sedate and supremely cheap, and grudgingly accept that they cannot maintain the lifestyle that ought to go with the value of their properties, which have risen along with Marbella's popularity. But then everything is relative: Sheik Yamani probably doesn't have a pension.

HOTEL Los Monteros

A luxury beach club hotel, Los Monteros consists almost entirely of small suites instead of rooms, and is situated amongst the lush vegetation of a tropical garden on the main coast road just outside Marbella. The best rooms on the Mediterranean side overlook one of the hotel's two swimming pools, a splash away from a private beach, where the set lunch should satisfy the heartiest appetite. The main restaurant, the El Corzo grill, has marvellous poultry and fish specialities. Indeed the hotel's only drawback is the price, high enough for the owners to throw in a free champagne cocktail party for the guests once a week.

GRANADA

The Moorish Kings who created the masterpiece of the Alhambra – the Arabic word for the 'red palace' – were archaeological vandals. Each ruler did not attempt to improve on his predecessors work; he simply tore most of it down and constructed something else in its place. The royal palace of the Alhambra, accordingly, was not built of rock and marble, but largely out of brick rubble, a whim of the moment by King Abul Hachach Yusuf II in the 14th century. He could afford to build so delicate a pavilion because one of his predecessors, Ibn Ahmar, had moved the River Darro several miles to give the Alhambra both serenity and a permanent water supply, safely inside its outer perimeter of huge walls and towers. From the right bank of the Darro, on St Nicholas's Terrace in the Albaicín quarter, there is a superb view of the Alhambra at sunset.

The survival of this medieval Arab palace was due to historical accident. Divisions among the ruling Moorish families forced the

Alhambra

last Arab ruler of Granada, Boabdil, to hand over the keys of the city in 1492 to the advancing Catholic armies of Ferdinand and Isabella, whose marriage had united Christian Spain. Boabdil rode away in tears of despair until rounded upon by his mother. 'Do not let me hear you weeping like a woman', she said, 'for what you could not defend like a man.' It was a happy chance that Ferdinand and Isabella appreciated the Alhambra's wonderful use of light and space, and instead of destroying it, had it fully restored. Even during the violent occupation by the French troops of Napoleon, the Alhambra rose above the conflict. It somehow inspired a French lieutenant to defy an order, handed to him directly by one of Napoleon's marshals, to supervise the Alhambra's destruction – on impulse he put out the burning fuses himself.

The problem with the Alhambra is that every tourist in Spain wants to see it and on some days it seems as if all of them are there. Even arriving when it opens, usually at 9 am, is no guarantee that you will not be swamped by the first coachloads of tourists before you leave. There is, however, an answer. During the summer months, on fête days and on the evenings before fête days, and on Saturdays, the Alhambra is floodlit. On some of these days, though not on all, visits are restricted to groups of at least 25 people. They will be simple enough to join, and far fewer than the massed crowds of the daytime. They are also relatively easy to lose, and you can then go round on your own, and appreciate the beauty of one of the true wonders of the world.

HOTEL Parador Nacional de San Francisco

If you intend to see the Alhambra at its best, arriving early in the morning or late in the evening, then staying nearby is quite essential. This government inn, with superb views of the Generalife (the summer palace of the Sultans) was built in the gardens of a Franciscan monastery. Although the food may leave something to be desired, the rooms are all air-conditioned and with bath, and the setting is marvellous. But book six months in advance.

SEVILLE

The Sevillians never believe in doing anything by halves. When, no longer under Moorish rule, they replaced the great mosque with a church, they pulled down most of it and built in its place the largest gothic cathedral in Christendom. A gloomy building of vast proportions, it has an organ to match that can produce a cacaphony of sounds which would not seem out of place in the *1812 Overture*. But the Christians could not quite bring themselves to destroy the minaret of the mosque, Giralda, known as the 'weather-vane' because of the revolving bronze statue on its top. It is ironical, though, that the call to Mass comes from a Moorish tower.

King Ferdinand, who in 1248 defeated the Moors, had his own way of dealing with non-believers. He did not stop short of personally kindling the fire on which heretics were burned, holding prayers for their souls before starting their funeral pyre. He was, however, a relatively merciful king if compared to an earlier Moorish ruler, al-Mutadid, who kept a harem of more than 800 women, and sawed off the heads of several of his courtiers who dared even to look at his concubines, using their upturned skulls as macabre flower pots. It would have taken a truly brutal monarch to upstage al-Mutadid, and sure enough one did – the aptly named Pedro the Cruel. When he failed to seduce a lady of the court, Pedro had her burned to death, along with her personal maid.

In later centuries the equally unpleasant Spanish Inquisition spread to the New World as the voyages of discovery crossed the Atlantic. It was from Seville that Amerigo Vespucci set off to find, and give his name to, America; and that Magellan began the first circumnavigation of the globe.

It is, perhaps, this background of passion and persecution that makes Seville's spring festival both a pious and a frenetic occasion. Counting rehearsals, the Holy Week celebrations last a full nine days; the first official procession is on Palm Sunday and the last disappearing into the sunset on Good Friday.

Seville's Spring Fair

To the outside observer, these processions are a mixture of the sacred and the profane. In one, devout women wear real crowns of thorns, and their own blood splashes on their white clothing. Men doing penance stagger through the streets carrying huge wooden crosses reminiscent of what we imagine to have been the scene before the Crucifixion. People prostrate themselves in front of the Madonna in the Cathedral, thrusting their fingers into the wounds in the statue of Christ to aid their salvation. Women weep at the sight of the Macarena, the Virgin of Hope, and sing long laments devoted to the suffering of Christ. But every so often the mood changes from sombre to exultant, when dark-haired Spanish ladies with flashing eyes and lovely ankles parade in marvellous dresses and flowing shawls. Bullfighting is a major form of entertainment for the Sevillians, and their favourite fighters parade arrogantly in the streets, like a circus coming to town. Add to this gypsies with breathtaking dances, the unending explosion of firecrackers, and a march of mummers dressed up as Roman centurions – a reminder perhaps that this was also the birthplace of the Emperor Trajan – and you have an altogether incongruous yet fascinating spectacle.

Holy Week and the Spring Fair was once noted for its lavish parties catering for thousands of guests in the courtyards of magnificent villas. Such parties still go on, but more discreetly, in a Spain where conspicuous consumption is likely to receive public criticism. Nowadays Holy Week has more of a common touch, with the young, the poor and the unemployed just as prepared to stay up all night, every night, sometimes those who have to go to work literally sleeping on the job. When the city of Carmen and Don Juan finally pauses for breath, the cafés are full of flamenco dancers, emotionally drained and physically exhausted, having given their all to keep the spirit of Andalucia safe for another year.

El Alcazar: palace of Pedro the Cruel

Visitors to Seville in April for Holy Week and the Spring Fair need stamina. Although of course it is possible to opt out of the celebrations before dawn, few hotel rooms are entirely insulated against the sound of the 'sevillanas', played and danced in the lavish pavilions set up along the main procession route. Temporary stands provide vantage points on the Real de la Feria to watch the processions although, even if you manage to buy some tickets, do not be surprised to find someone else in your seats. Overbooking is not the exclusive province of airlines and hotels, it seems. Many streets are closed during the festivities and getting about on foot is the only practical solution. Booking hotel accommodation several months in advance is more or less essential.

Even if you are unable to visit Seville during April, the city has some remarkable buildings worth a long journey to see. Perhaps one of the best to visit, if only because it has relatively few visitors, is the Casa de Pilatos, Pilate's house, built by the Marquis of Tarifa in 1540. The Marquis, a devout Christian, had paced out the distance from the real Pontius Pilate's house in Jerusalem to the hill of the Crucifixion, which resembled a hill outside Seville. The Marquis measured the same number of steps back into the city, and built his house on the spot, a breathtaking blend of Renaissance and Moorish styles, around a vast courtyard with a huge marble fountain. It will be less simple to avoid large crowds in the Cathedral or the beautiful palace of the Alcazar. Seville also has treasures of a different kind: the Archives of the Indies, including many private letters of Christopher Columbus, which can be seen nearby.

HOTEL Alfonso XIII

The hotel Alfonso XIII was formerly called the Andalucia Palace, which is worth knowing because some taxi drivers still call it by that name. Although opened by King Alfonso himself in 1928, it looks very much like an old palace, with Moorish decor and sumptuous furnishings. Everything is on a epic scale, huge public rooms, big bedrooms, grand bathrooms where even the toilet roll holders are marble. The miles of plushly carpeted corridors may help to explain why room service gives a new dimension to the word 'manyana'. However, the gardens are delightful, the swimming pool superb, and the centre of Seville only a few minutes away.

VALENCIA

Much of Spain is barren, inhospitable country, bereft of water beneath a fierce burning sun. These were familiar obstacles to the Arab army of the Prophet, which in 711 AD began an invasion that was to take them in less than 25 years across Spain and to the gates of Poitiers in France. Religious fanatics they may have been, but the Moors were formidable fighting men, equally skilled on foot and on horseback, with archers of frightening accuracy. Their shock troops were the legendary Berbers of Yusuf, who went into battle with a crescendo of drums, to frighten the horses of their opponents.

It would take an outstanding fighter to defeat the Moors, and Spain found him in Rodrigo Diaz of Vivar, El Cid, a name derived from Cidi, an Arabic word meaning lord or master. Rodrigo, a Castillian originally in the service of his local king, Sancho II, was little more than a mercenary who fought for either Christian or Moor as the mood took him. What concrete evidence there is of his character shows him to have been proud, selfish and cruel, capable of destroying nine horses in a single afternoon while fighting bulls from horseback, his private obsession. He was exiled by Alfonso VI in 1081, fought for the Moorish King of Zaragoza, then again for Alfonso in the famous siege of Valencia in which El Cid is supposed to have brought the final collapse of a starving garrison by using his catapults to shoot, not rocks, but loaves of bread over the walls.

El Cid held Valencia for five years, but was mortally wounded in a skirmish near the city, and the Moors confidently expected its capitulation. To their horror, however, El Cid reappeared at the head of his knights in full armour, riding his favourite charger. The claims of the sultans that this was a trick, that they were being attacked by a dead man held in place on his horse by ropes and leathers, only terrified their superstitious troops even more. They fled from the battlefield, leaving Valencia secure in the hands of El Cid's widow, who had been ordered by her

Effigies of the unpopular burn on the fallas

husband that, living or dead, he must lead his men to victory.

HOTELS

Monte Picayo

At Puzol, ten miles north of Valencia, this is a sophisticated hotel set in an orange grove. Most of the rooms have balconies with views of the sea, which is about two miles away. There is a large swimming pool in the grounds, and a night club and casino. Not the place to be if on a budget.

Luis Vives

At El Saler, 14 miles south of Valencia, near Spain's largest lake, Lake Albufera, splendid for boating and fishing; even closer to the sea, with a long sandy beach running into the hotel grounds. Luis Vives is a parador, with modern but beautiful arcaded terraces, and has a fine restaurant and a large swimming pool.

For seven days each year Valencia holds a splendid carnival, which reaches its climax on March 19. This is the famous 'fallas', bonfires on which effigies are burnt, a practice that goes back to the Middle Ages when the craft union of carpenters burned the wood shavings accumulated over many months of work in 'fallas' (from the Latin 'facula' or 'torch'). As the festival developed, the burning objects began to include effigies of unpopular people made of pasteboard and paper maché.

As the figures grew bigger and bigger, the rivalry to produce floats on which to carry them in procession became fiercer every year, so much so that in modern times they are sheer works of art, huge and hugely satirical. The targets of their satire are famous Spanish personalities, no longer limited to Valencia, with politicians to the fore. In the days of General Franco, when there was no freedom of speech, the Valencians even included him in their festival and ridiculed him with impunity. After days of festivities, the floats and effigies are burned on the night of San José.

——————PAMPLONA——————

Religion, chivalry and cruelty are woven inextricably into the fabric of Spanish history and the philosophy of its people. Which is why, perhaps, Ignacio Loyola, a young noble caught up in one of the complicated causes of medieval politics, saw no contradiction in abandoning his sword in favour of a bible. Struck by an arrow during the bloody but unsuccessful attack on Pamplona, in 1521, he spent several months recovering from his wounds. It was a time for spiritual contemplation and, followed by a pilgrimage to Jerusalem, led eventually to the founding of the Jesuit movement of which Loyola became the first Vicar-General.

The pavement in San Ignacio Street has a plaque marking the spot where Loyola fell and became Pamplona's most famous visitor, conveniently overlooking the fact that their beleaguered defenders had done their best to kill him, and he to kill them, in a siege that, even in a cruel age, was noted for its appalling atrocities.

Pamplona commanded two major routes to the frontier, the Roncesvalles and Vellate

St Ignacio Loyola

Passes, and was a strategic objective for centuries. The capital of the ancient Pyrenean kingdom of Navarre, lying on a plateau on the banks of the Arga River, it is said to have been founded by the Roman general Pompey. Pamplona was taken by the Moors, and delivered by the Emperor Charlemagne, who promptly rendered it defenceless by dismantling the city walls. Over the centuries, the citizens of Pamplona have learned not to trust their friends.

Yet despite the imposing gothic cathedral with its perfectly formed cloister, and the maze of little medieval streets hugging its walls, Pamplona would remain a city of only passing interest but for the extraordinary festival of San Fermin, the Running of the Bulls.

Although the Spanish bull has its origins in the wild bulls of North Africa, which had a ritual purpose in ancient Carthage, the bull bred for the ring is not some hereditary accident. Bull-breeding ranches are big business in Spain. The Spanish fighting bull is a product of a selective process which begins with his parentage and ends with an exercise to discover his aggressive instincts on ranches deep in the wilds. Here ranchers on horseback test bulls in private rings to ensure that only the most formidable are taken to the public corrals. The final selection is made by the bullfighter and his representatives, who know that a bull lacking courage can only make the task more difficult in the ring. The best bulls are, therefore, animals of huge speed and power, naked aggression and an obsessive instinct to kill.

The first time even the Pamplona public usually sees these bulls is in the ring, except during the 'encierros', the running of the bulls from the corrals to the ring. At eight o'clock each morning of the festival, the bulls are released from a pen near the Plaza San Domingo, escorted by the more reckless local inhabitants, mainly the young men of Navarre out to prove their manhood to the watching senoritas. In confined streets, barricaded off to prevent the bulls getting loose in the rest of the city, some daring young men do capeless passes and finesses in front of the sharp horns. Others run the gauntlet of the course, trying to out-pace an animal becoming more dangerous and street-wise with every moment.

A few foolhardy tourists, lacking even the rudiments of caping bulls, try to emulate them, often with disastrous results. Considering the near-suicidal risks, it is remarkable that more people are not killed or seriously injured. Those who escape unscathed claim that the experience is exhilarating beyond belief. In other words, great fun for the survivors.

The men who will kill the bulls, in the afternoon, dislike the Pamplona festival. Most bulls released into the ring will never have seen a man before and will take precious minutes to discover that the toreador, not his cape, is the real enemy. To the Pamplona bull, the man has already become a familiar (and tempting) target.

The best, and safest, place to watch the running of the bulls is in the Plaza San Domingo, but visitors need to be in position extremely early, perhaps at 5.30 am to be sure of a good spot. Rooms along the route are rented out at exorbitant prices (the hotel porter always seems to have a cousin); the best are those on the first floor with a balcony. If you intend to stay in Pamplona for the festival, which usually begins on July 7, it is essential to book many months in advance; expect hotel prices to be correspondingly inflated. The town is extremely noisy, with festivities far into the night, so uninterrupted sleep is unlikely. Pickpockets have a field day.

HOTEL Tres Reyes

Beautiful wooded surroundings and a fine swimming pool are the outstanding features of this luxurious hotel, where the food and service are exceptional. It is, however, rather large – it has 168 superbly appointed bedrooms – and a little impersonal.

The bulls of Pamplona

LOIRE

It is an unpalatable, yet undeniable, fact that when the English were finally thrown out of France, the great age of the Loire and her châteaux began. The Loire valley became the favourite region of the Valois kings and their courtiers and fortresses were turned into elegant palaces. Charles VIII and François I fell under the spell of the Italian Renaissance, and the Italian artists, architects and craftsmen achieved with the mind what the English had failed to do with the sword. Château after château fell under the Italian influence. François I even brought Leonardo da Vinci, the greatest artist of them all, to Amboise. Despite the turmoil of the Religious Wars which followed this century of peace, some of the masterpieces they created survive to this day.

The visitor is so spoilt for choice that certain ground rules need to be applied to make the best use of the time available. Unless you speak reasonable French and can travel outside the summer peak (although the châteaux are at their best in summer), a guided and largely incomprehensible tour, crocodile fashion, can be immensely frustrating. Only a quite brilliant château can compensate for the freedom to wander at will.

Happily, the most outstanding château of all comes into that category – Chenonceaux, which has no guided tours, plenty of information in English and, in July and August, even a children's nursery.

Re-built in the 16th century by the royal tax collector, Thomas Bohier, the original château of Chenonceaux had been owned by the impoverished Marques family, who were compelled to sell off their land piece by piece to avoid financial ruin. Bohier achieved such a stranglehold on the estate that the final piece, the château itself, was comparatively cheap. Bohier had married money, and his wife, Catherine Briçonnet, was a great influence on the new château's design. It was always coveted by François I, and after the death of the Bohiers, he had the tax accounts examined, and used them as an excuse to seize Chenonceaux for himself. When the next king, Henry II, gave the château to his famous mistress, Diane de Poitiers, the first extension was built on a bridge over the river Cher – a striking and imaginative creation, audacious in its age. Diane de Poitiers was, by all accounts, a remarkable woman. She was 20 years older than the King, looked 30 when in fact in her middle 50s, and is reputed to have taken mysterious drugs to maintain her appearance. The sexual favours she bestowed on the king might well have kept her in a position of power for much longer, had not Henry been killed by an accidental lance-thrust in a jousting tournament in 1559. His widow, Catherine de Medici, saw her chance for revenge, and forced Diane to give up Chenonceaux in exchange for another, much gloomier, château – Chaumont. It was Catherine who added the upper stories to the bridge at Chenonceaux to create an architectural masterpiece. The dispute between the two women, however, ended unhappily for both. Diane refused to live at Chaumont and spent her final years at the relatively obscure château of Anet. Catherine herself spent some time at Chaumont, dabbling in the occult in a sinister room at the top of a tower with her astrologer, Ruggieri. It is said that, in this turret room, Catherine was given a glimpse of the future, which foretold the premature deaths of her three sons, François II, Charles IX and Henry III, and the end of the Valois line.

Another château to which there is easy access is Chambord. When François I decided to build himself a hunting lodge for the odd weekend, he did nothing by halves, which is why Chambord is 170 yards in length and 130 yards wide and has 440 rooms; and the River Cosson was diverted by more than a mile to improve its setting. Although Chambord is now completely unfurnished, an empty shell with echoes of past glory, its sheer size stuns the senses. It has its own architectural masterpiece, one that reflects the intrigue of the period – a double-spiral staircase so cleverly designed that one person could ascend and another descend, simultaneously, without seeing one another. Although there is no positive evidence, it may have been designed by Leonardo da Vinci himself. Visitors can wander about the château at will.

The Château de Cheverny is a complete contrast to Chambord because it was constructed in the Classical style in one period of the 17th century, with no afterthoughts, and has remained in the possession of a single French family. The furnishings, therefore, reflect the life of a French lord through the centuries, and the château has a warmth and sense of purpose. Its principal curiosity is a hunting museum with a collection of some two thousand sets of antlers; so it was evidently not a healthy place to be a deer. There are no guided tours in English, but visitors can opt to go around on their own.

Diane de Poitiers

Château de Chambord

The fourth château without which no visit to the Loire would be complete is Villandry, although only for its formal 16th-century gardens, brilliantly restored by its 19th-century owner, Dr Carvallo. There are three great terraces, with the dominant themes of water, ornaments and plants; from the last we can deduce that many of the flowers and vegetables of today were already known. A conspicuous exception was the potato, which did not reach France on any scale until Parmentier introduced it in the 18th century, even though it had arrived in Spain from South America much earlier, appearing in the accounts of a Seville hospital in 1573. Even without the potato, the grounds of Villandry show how sophisticated gardening had already become and, visually, they are a masterpiece.

At other châteaux, visitors are rather more restricted. At Amboise, a massive château rising high above the town, the Italian influence first manifested itself – a movement that ultimately resulted in Leonardo da Vinci taking up residence as a kind of royal architect, and remaining there until his death. One of its most distinguished features is the Minimes Tower, constructed with a spiral ramp so that mounted horsemen could ride up to the first floor. In practice, it proved rather hazardous, as the Emperor Charles V discovered on visiting François I. Tapestries overhanging the ramp caught fire, Charles fell off his horse, and was all but suffocated in the panic and confusion that followed.

The exterior of Blois, another massive château, is more interesting than its interior, to which there are occasional guided tours in English. You can see the marvellous octagonal staircase constructed under François I, and Catherine de Medici's room, 237 carved wood panels full of secret compartments which no doubt contained state papers, jewellery and, possibly, poisons. The Queen used more orthodox methods to persuade her son, Henry III, to have her principal rival for power, the Duke of Guise, murdered in 1588. Henry only agreed to such a desperate measure because the Duke, Lieutenant-General of the Kingdom, had engineered the recall of the French Parliament, the States-General, whose deputies were bent on removing the King himself. He used a meeting of the royal council to lure the Duke into his bedroom, where no fewer than 20 assassins lay in wait. Even then the Duke, who was tremendously strong, disabled five of them and dragged a dozen more across the room before succumbing to

Octagonal staircase at Blois

his wounds. Henry did not ·have long to savour his triumph: eight months later he too fell to an assassin's dagger.

Many other châteaux are worth a visit on a longer, or second, trip to the Loire. They include Chinon, fortified by Richard the Lionheart, but the town, where Joan of Arc first met ·the Dauphin, is more interesting than the castle ruins. For a beautiful château still occupied by the family that built it, visit Montgeoffroy, near Beaufort-en-Vallée. For relief from hordes of visitors, try the Château of Montrésor, built in the 15th century by the Count of Anjou, Foulques Nerra, a man who alternated between bloody deeds and acts of repentance. For a castle with riverside views, look at Montsoreau, the setting for a Dumas novel. For a moated castle, half mansion half medieval fortress, go to Sully-sur-Loire, if only to see the incredible timber roof of the great hall, constructed in chestnut in the 14th century. For the shortest visit of all, look at Azay-le-Rideau, an exquisitely designed Renaissance château. But don't bother to go in: the interior is an enormous anti-climax.

Most châteaux are open every day during the summer months, from about 9 am to 5 pm, but are closed for lunch from noon to 2 pm. The best time to visit is as early as possible in the morning.

HOTEL Château d'Artigny

A shameless fake, completed during the First World War by the perfume millionaire, François Coty, this 18th-century-style castle turned hotel is situated some seven miles from Tours, and is an ideal base for exploring genuine châteaux country. Even if the château is not authentic, no expense has been spared to give the visitor a feeling of secluded elegance in manorial surroundings. All the rooms in the château have private facilities, though some are rather poky (and beware the annexe). The food, while expensive, is outstanding, which is just as well, because the nearest alternative restaurant is miles away. The grounds are marvellous, and include a heated swimming pool.

Renting a château

Visiting a château is an enormously popular pastime and staying overnight in a château turned into a first-class hotel has become increasingly common; but few people would contemplate the idea of renting an entire château for themselves. Yet more and more of these huge and splendid structures are now available for much of the year, and at prices which are certainly not beyond the pocket of many would-be holidaymakers.

Of course few families on their own want a vast house with perhaps 20 or more rooms at their disposal. However by sharing with friends, they can achieve an undreamed of economy of scale, and get far more for their money than they would in much smaller properties.

The snag of course is organising such an arrangement. The choice of with whom you share is of vital importance. Do you really know them well enough to spend 24 hours a day with them (and possibly their children) for a fortnight or longer? Multiple sharing arrangements involving couples can be even more difficult, leading, as Russell Harty once described vividly in a Sunday newspaper article, to ludicrous levels of competition, over who had swum the most lengths of the pool or achieved the highest gastronomic heights.

The common denominator in most disputes is money, so any sharing must be placed on a professional basis from the start. Persuade all the parties involved to accept one person to handle all the financial arrangements. They should keep a proper set of accounts so that everyone can see exactly what has been, and will be, spent. However honest and well-intentioned, people have been known to get into a muddle about shared costs of ferry bookings, motorail, insurance, deposits, etc., often ending with the worst of both worlds – out of pocket and under· suspicion of having exaggerated the costs. Once abroad, the only way to operate a sharing arrangement fairly is to have a kitty into which everyone contributes regularly, and which is used to pay for any 'pooled' item, such as petrol, food or drink. Everything should be written down, so that any thought of unfairness can be entirely eliminated. Every group of holiday-makers that rejects the idea of a precise system in the mistaken belief that they and their friends are above such petty disputes, end in vowing never to have a shared holiday again without it.

A château or large country house has many advantages. Some are so big that families do not have to live in one another's pockets; the less close the contact, invariably the less the friction, although even the largest houses rarely have more than one kitchen.

In the past there have been two problems, quality and access. Many large houses have been terribly run down, and really not fit to live in, even for a fortnight's holiday. However owners are now being encouraged to spend money on renovation, so that at least part of the château is clean and properly furnished. On their side, owners have experienced, or heard of, problems in renting to people outside their own country, and have been reluctant to make their properties available internationally. Some of those difficulties have been overcome by Nicholas Brindlecombe of *Vacances en Campagne*, who has put together the first complete brochure of châteaux to rent. In France, there should be no shortage of choice, because some 6,000 are still inhabited, and only 600 of those are formally open to the public.

It is even possible to rent a château in the Loire Valley. Le Mont Suzey at Solonge, half an hour's drive from Blois, was built in Norman style in the 19th century. It has an enormous drawing room complete with grand piano and billiard table, 12 bedrooms, and a swimming pool in the wooded grounds.

Another château with a swimming pool is Château d'Azy, situated just outside St Benin d'Azy, on the borders of Burgundy. Built in Renaissance style in the 19th century, complete with marvellous pointed turrets, it is now owned by the Princess de Croy, who has an apartment in one wing. But this still leaves enough of the château to sleep 16 people. There is a snag – it has no kitchen, so meals have to be brought in from outside.

There is a kitchen, modern and well-equipped, in the Château de Crazannes, north of Bordeaux, not far from the Atlantic coast. Indeed, the whole château, which dates back to the 14th century, has been completely renovated regardless of expense and sleeps 12 in exceptional comfort. Set in some 20 acres of parkland, it has a beautiful terrace overlooking a moat.

For a genuine castle, in the English sense of the word, one with real dungeons, you have to cross into Italy, to the Castello Theodoli, at Ciciliano. It belongs to the Theodoli family, one of whose ancestors was a wheelwright knighted for his services to the Emperor Charlemagne during a battle in the ninth century, when apparently he completed a wheel change on the Emperor's chariot faster than could be managed in the pits at Monza. The castle is some ten miles from Hadrian's villa at Tivoli, and within easy reach of Rome. It sleeps 12 comfortably in vast bedrooms. Two or three families could easily avoid each other for several days. A cleaning lady comes with the castle, which was built in the 12th century. It still has its original front door key, which is seven inches long, and turns a vast lock in even vaster double doors. You half expect a pantomime giant to appear at any moment.

Château Lasalle, on a working estate, is probably the southernmost château available for rent in France.

PARIS: MÉTRO-LAND

The true métro-land, begging Sir John Betjeman's pardon, is not that stretch of the Metro Line on the London Underground which, believe it or not, once took city workers home to green fields, but the best way for visitors to see Paris. Driving around in one's own car, in the daytime, is little short of hopeless, because of the lack of parking spaces. Buses are increasingly becoming victims of bigger and bigger traffic jams and the numbers recording francs on taxi meters seem to move at a speed roughly equivalent to a fruit machine in motion. The answer, then, is to go below, into Métro-land, where the Métro, short for Métropolitan, is fast, cheap and easy to use.

Entrance to the Métro

Most British visitors to Paris probably have some experience of the London Underground; they will find the Paris Métro an improvement. To start with, it is considerably less expensive, because it receives a huge subsidy, largely financed by a tax on Parisian businesses, based on the logic that most users of the system, even allowing for tourists, will be going to work. Unlike London, there is no complicated price zoning system, but a flat rate fare for the journey, however far. The only exception is the R.E.R., a rapid urban transport system closely linked to the Métro, but of little use to the visitor unless he or she is crossing from one side of Paris to the other.

No-one, other than the unenlightened tourist, buys a single ticket for the Métro, which is uneconomic and time-consuming. At the very least, they ask for un carnet, a batch of ten tickets priced at a discount. For visitors, billets de tourisme valid for two or four days are also available, which allow unlimited bus travel, the use of the funiculaire in Montmartre as often as you like, and first-class travel anywhere on the Métro. Yes the Métro, unlike the London underground, has two classes of travel. First class can be a sensible extravagance during the rush hours, which start earlier and go on later in Paris, when second-class can be extremely crowded. Do not, however, be tempted to travel first class with a second-class ticket – frequent checks are made, and the fines can be extremely heavy.

In first class, you obviously need to keep your ticket to show that you are entitled to be there. In second class, a great many Parisians still throw away their ticket through sheer force of habit, despite the efforts of the authorities to make them hang on to them, as a means of reducing fraudulent travel. Tickets are not collected at the end of your journey, so apart from spot checks, once they are in the system, there is little risk of fare dodgers being caught. As a result, Paris has the most athletic passengers in the world, renowned for their ability to leap over barriers and travel for nothing.

However one other athletic pursuit on the Métro has almost disappeared. In the old days almost every station had a pneumatic barrier to the platform; it closed as the train arrived, avoiding the traditional British pastime of keeping one of the Underground train doors open by fair means or foul, and squeezing in. Pitting your strength against the pneumatic barrier was great sport, but most of them have now been removed.

Even so, the Métro does offer demanding

exercise if you attempt a journey that involves changing from one line to another. This is one aspect of the Parisian system, perhaps the only aspect, which leaves a great deal to be desired. The distances between one line and the next are truly immense, a maze of corridors and staircases, until you begin to wonder if you have not perhaps made a dreadful mistake, and that you are not joining another line, but actually walking underground to the next station.

Using the system is, however, extremely simple. Like London, the trains all carry their final destination on the front so that you can see the direction in which you are travelling. But unlike London, all the stations and all the passageways leading to and from the platforms carry the name of the terminus on the line they serve. If you keep this in mind, it is almost impossible, as many people do in London, to find yourself travelling in the wrong direction.

As no part of Paris is more than a few hundred yards from a Métro station, all the major tourist attractions are within easy access. But beware the obvious: the Champs-Élysées station, for example, is not really the best starting point to absorb the atmosphere of the most famous street in Paris. From the Charles de Gaulle-Étoile station, you can stroll, downhill, the full length of the Avenue, through the Place de la Concorde, once the home of the Guillotine but now just a giant-size dodgem track, and equally deadly; and finally into the royal gardens of the Tuileries.

The most familiar landmark in Paris, the Eiffel Tower, curiously does not have its own Métro station, nor indeed one that is particularly convenient. The most agreeable approach is by way of Trocadéro Station (named by the way, for those who like to know these things, after a little fort outside Cadiz, heroically captured by the French in 1823) through the Trocadéro Gardens, and across the Pont d'Iena. As the ground falls away sharply, the Eiffel Tower comes into

The Métro

view, as it were, from the top downwards, a rather startling sight.

Most newcomers to Paris feel a compulsion to ascend the Eiffel Tower. They should know that the queues are often enormous, the cost of going right to the top prohibitive, and the view, other than on an extremely clear day, not as impressive as from other places in Paris. From, for example, the top of the Cathedral of Nôtre Dame, which is almost directly opposite the Cité station, on the Isle de la Cité, the earliest inhabited part of Paris, in the middle of the River Seine. The bell tower is, however, an arduous climb.

The Louvre Museum does have its own station, with replicas of statues on the platform which would present an irresistable challenge to British vandals, but somehow survive intact in Paris. The Louvre is so vast that a dedicated visitor could spend an entire week inside, apart, that is, from the inconvenient fact that it is closed every Tuesday. The busiest day is Sunday, when admission is free. All bags have to be checked in, but there is no charge, making the Louvre left-luggage office the most convenient and

HOTEL The Ritz

When the French novelist Marcel Proust died in 1922, his final words were a complaint about the service at The Ritz. Which was a trifle unfair, as, although not actually staying at the hotel at the time, Proust's last request had been for a glass of a rather obscure beer, chilled by the Ritz bartender. Even then, it might have arrived before Proust expired, had not the bartender refused to open the bottle until it was at exactly the right temperature.

The Ritz, then and now, has always seemed a little larger than life, ever since in 1898 the great hotelier Cesar Ritz transformed what had been a private house in the Place Vendôme into a hotel of ultimate luxury. His clients were largely the nobility of Europe, Russian counts and Italian princes, although almost anyone with the wherewithal would be accommodated in one of the 45 suites – in those days reserving simply a bedroom was almost unheard of, a social gaffe par excellence. One of the most frequent visitors was a German arms dealer who brought more than 200 pieces of handmade luggage of inordinant luxury and took a suite of five rooms, consisting of bedroom, sitting room, master bedroom, sitting room, and bedroom, in that order. He needed that amount of space to accommodate his two stunning mistresses who regularly accompanied him, adding a new dimension to the old saying, turn and turn about.

Edward VII was a regular visitor to the hotel, which installed an extra-large, waist-high marble bath – though whether because the corpulent monarch had become stuck in a normal-size bath, or whether because it was required to accommodate more than one person at a time, remains discreetly shrouded in mystery. At any rate, the ivory and gold bell pulls he used to summon either 'maid' or 'valet' are still there, and remain in use to this day.

You can still stay in the royal suite, now known as the Windsor Suite, because it was reserved for a continuous three-year period by the Duke and Duchess of Windsor after the Abdication, until a suitable permanent residence could be found for them in Paris. It has Louis XVIth furniture, 18th-century tapestries, Persian carpets, opulent decor overlooked by a portrait of the Duke himself, and a personal maid and butler constantly in attendance. All this will cost, including 15% service, some £3,500 for bed and breakfast. Amazingly enough, the suite has a 90% occupancy rate, although the average pre-war stay of ten days has gone down to three.

Every suite in the Ritz has been redecorated by its present owner, Egyptian businessman Mohamed Al-Fayed, who spent 30 million pounds buying the hotel and at least as much again on the interior. Gilt mirrors and gold clocks were acquired in such quantities that the refurbishment of the Ritz (still in progress) seriously distorted that section of the European antique market.

For a hotel with only 200 rooms, The Ritz has a huge staff, 430, including three chefs for their restaurant, the Espadon, whose food, ambience and quality of service is superior to Maxims or Le Tour d'Argent, or so say many French gourmets.

The Ritz of today would certainly meet with the approval of its founder, Cesar Ritz, who was responsible for so many innovations which have become permanent features of luxury hotel life, including king-size beds (originally and literally, for kings), wall lights, white ties for waiters and black suits for head waiters. Try as they may, no hotel is able to emulate The Ritz: it is simply in a class by itself.

Salon of the Imperial Suite at the Ritz

cheapest in Paris.

You can therefore shop with impunity two Métro stops away (look for the Opéra station) in the Boulevard Haussmann, home of the huge department stores, Galeries Lafayette and Au Printemps, which is so enormous that it has spread into three buildings, separated by a pedestrian street. If you want a coffee or a drink after shopping, back in the Place de l'Opéra is the Café de la Paix. It is by no means cheap, but it has a marvellous atmosphere, and is still a fashionable place for Parisians to see or be seen.

For less expensive items, though frankly fewer and fewer bargains, the Paris flea market, the Marché aux Puces, is a few minutes walk north of a Métro terminus station, Porte de Clignancourt, and open from Saturday to Monday. Also in the north of Paris is Montmartre, with the illuminated windmill of the Moulin Rouge club revolving on the edge of the Place de Pigalle. Much of the night life in the district around Pigalle station is, however, extremely seedy, making one wonder what the original Jean-Baptiste Pigalle would have thought of it all as, far from being the Paul Raymond of Montmartre, he was actually a carver of majestic tombstones . . . come to think of it, not entirely inappropriate.

The nearest station to the funiculaire of Montmartre is in fact Abbesses, named after the last Abbesse de Montmorency-Laval, who went to her death during the French Revolution without revealing the hiding place of her convent's treasure, which may have been buried in the convent grounds on the site of the present Métro. Some mysterious accidents occurred during the excavations for the station, and the headless ghost of the abbess is said to walk the station at night.

At the top of the funiculaire is the beautiful white basilica of Sacré-Coeur, and from its steps an exceptional view of the city, best seen at sunset. However, the atmosphere is less enchanting in the Place du Tertre, the heart of Montmartre, which is frequently packed almost to bursting point with tourists. It is so crowded that no serious artist would

be seen dead in the place. Most of them, including Picasso and Toulouse-Lautrec, established themselves in Montparnasse in the south of Paris many decades ago. The Métro there is Montparnasse-Bienvenue, named belatedly after Jacques Bienvenue. As he was the engineer who created the system, they might have given him a station to himself.

The maps outside the Métro stations, be they in Montparnasse or Montmartre, seem to have been deliberately designed to confuse visitors, as the lines are imposed on a map of the city and extremely difficult to follow. A British engineer recently had the bright idea of converting a map of the Paris Métro system largely into straight lines like the familiar plan of the London Underground, and sent his design to the Paris Transport Department. It was rejected without hesitation, but then Parisians disapprove of those who tamper with tradition.

If the Métro gives you a taste for further underground experiences, it is possible to visit the sewers of Paris, a remarkable network of passageways and tunnels laid out by the engineer Eugène Belgrand in the middle of the last century. The point of entry is just to the east of the southern end of the Pont de l'Alma, two bridges east of the Eiffel Tower. Visiting times are between 2 and 5 pm on Mondays, Wednesdays and on the last Saturday of the month; but not if it is raining. The nearest Métro is Alma-Marceau, just north of Pont de l'Alma.

A rather more macabre experience is offered by a tour of the catacombs, a series of underground quarries dating from Roman times, which were turned, in the 1780s, into a charnel house for human skeletons removed from disused graveyards. Most of the victims of the Guillotine during the French Revolution eventually ended up in the Catacombs, which were also the headquarters of the French Resistance during the Second World War. The point of entry is a small pavilion on the south-west corner of the Place Denfert-Rochereau, in the south of Paris. The tour, through galleries lined with bones and skulls, takes place between 2 and 4 pm every day except Mondays, with additional tours at weekends between 9 and 11 am. The nearest Métro is Denfert-Rochereau.

CHAPTER 2

TRAINS TO TEMPT YOU

——— ORIENT EXPRESS ———

One evening in October, 1983, no fewer than three trains claiming to be the Orient Express left the Gare de l'Est in Paris. One of them was the genuine article, one a special centenary run on the original route and one the regular luxurious service on its way between London and Venice. When deciding to take a trip on the Orient Express, rail enthusiasts must be careful to define their requirements.

The genuine Orient Express died a death in May, 1977, when for most of the week the only way to reach Istanbul was in a second-class through car which took the best part of three days without a sleeping compartment or a restaurant car in sight. The train frequently arrived many hours late and was the supreme railway endurance test, the Matterhorn of the European railway system. Apart from the occasional exercise in private enterprise by a Bulgarian conductor, it was impossible to obtain as much as a cup of coffee on the way, so taking your own food and drink for the whole journey was essential.

The service was then mysteriously revived and upgraded, the result, it is said, of a diplomatic protest by the Rumanian Embassy in Paris, whose luckless diplomats are often forbidden for economy reasons to travel by air – or perhaps because what they are carrying in diplomatic bags might cause security alarms at airports to go beserk. In any event, Rumanian diplomats seem to be the only regular clientele on the daily run, which has only two coaches (first- and second-class sleeping cars) tacked on to the night train to Vienna and then on to other trains down into Eastern Europe. Although the train leaves from Paris too late for dinner, it does have a restaurant car attached in Hungary and Rumania, which is sheer luxury when compared to what was on offer in the 1970s. For any passengers hoping for excitement and intrigue, there is, alas, not a Mata Hari in sight.

The genuine Orient Express ends its run at Bucharest, which has a ring of authenticity about it, as the original train went only 45 miles further, to Giurgui. Giurgui was no Clapham Junction of the Balkans, but simply where the track reached the Danube. Georges Nagelmackers, creator of the original Orient Express and the Wagon Lit Company, had glossed over this inconvenient little fact when starting the service on October 4, 1883. Although the passengers were aware of the possibility of being attacked by bandits, and arrived at the Gare de l'Est bristling with weapons, they had no idea of the disagreeable journey that lay ahead of them. At Giurgui they had to cross the Danube by ferry and join a local train, then take horse-drawn coaches controlled by a ferocious-looking driver called Brankovits over what could easily have been a Transylvanian pass (and, dear Count Dracula, after dark). Another local train took them to Varna, where the line ran out altogether, leaving the journey to Istanbul to be completed by a none too salubrious boat on the Black Sea.

The shock of the later stages of the journey must have been made all the more traumatic by the luxury of the Orient Express rolling stock, which included a smoking car for the gentlemen, a ladies' boudoir, and a well-

59

Smoking Lounge and Library of the Orient Express in 1886

stocked library. The bathrooms, at each end of the train, had floors of delicate mosaic and the showers had endless supplies of hot and cold water. In the sleeping compartments, the beds, all with sprung mattresses, folded back into inlaid panelling, leaving the passengers to recline in red leather armchairs on deep pile Turkish carpets. More leather enhanced the restaurant car, covering the entire ceiling. The meals were prepared by a master chef from Burgundy; five courses worthy of a Michelin rosette, with magnificent wines kept cool, in those pre-refrigerator days, by huge blocks of ice.

By the turn of the century, the Orient Express reached Istanbul by way of Vienna, Budapest, Belgrade, Nisch and Sofia, with the passengers cocooned in their own little world, baggage secure and passports largely unchecked for the duration of the journey. This was the beginning of the era of romance and intrigue that inspired Agatha Christie to write her *Murder on the Orient Express*, and there were, indeed, at least two mysterious deaths of government agents who fell from the train in Rumania, or, more probably, were pushed. Incredible though it may seem, a former President of France did fall out of the train while on his way to answer a call of nature, clad only in his pyjamas – he escaped with bruises but, not surprisingly, it took some time for him to persuade local officials that he really was who he claimed to be, and not an escaped lunatic. One eccentric known to have travelled on the train was King Boris of Bulgaria, who could not be prevented from driving it within his own borders. Boris disregarded signals set at red in his obsession with speed and, on one occasion, badly burned a fireman by forcing him to over-stoke the furnace, and left the poor man for dead beside the track in his anxiety to arrive on schedule in his capital, Sofia.

The most regular passenger was the international arms dealer, Sir Basil Zaharoff, who always took sleeping compartment No. 7. One night he was awakened by a knock on his door from a beautiful Spaniard, the Duchess of Marchena, who, desperate to escape from her mad husband, promptly eloped into Zaharoff's compartment. Zaharoff made an honest woman of her after the Duke's death, 38 years later.

Back in the 1880s, the Orient Express was certainly the exclusive province of the rich. For the price of two return tickets, about £250, you could pay a year's rent on a Mayfair house in London. A servant's fare was more than his annual wages.

The problems of running the centenary special of the Orient Express were immense. The authorities in Eastern Europe had to be persuaded to re-open sections of line no longer used by international trains, some of them in areas close to military establishments. For the first leg of the journey, the only working steam engine belonging to French Railways was brought into action. However, as all the facilities for re-filling boilers from water tanks or troughs under the lines had long been removed, its first stop at Château-Thierry lasted an hour while a posse of local fire engines re-filled it with their hoses.

This run over the old route was, however, a one-off affair. The London to Venice regular service, revived in May, 1982, began by running over part of the southern route to Istanbul, which in the 1920s was a mere 56 hours from Paris. The southern route became possible only after the construction of the remarkable Simplon tunnel, the longest of all the Alpine railway tunnels, opened in 1906. Its German engineers achieved what many thought to be impossible by the technique of spiral tunnelling from each end, surveying underground so accurately that the two ends of the tunnel met in the middle.

Alas, the revamped Venice Simplon Orient-Express, to give it the proper title, had to admit defeat when it came to steam as there was no way to operate a steam engine on this route in modern times. Curiously, the loco-motive, like the track, was always outside the

jurisdiction of the Orient Express Company which, throughout its long history, had never owned either. What the Simplon Orient Mark II did have was the most magnificent collection of railway carriages in the history of train travel.

The man who has made all this possible is James Sherwood, multi-millionaire chairman of Sea Containers, a shipping company speci-alising in container transport. Sherwood has put some of the company's profits to good use in buying up and restoring old Wagon Lit rolling stock, which had been scattered round Europe. One of the original Orient Express carriages had even been used as a brothel at Limoges. Perhaps not even James Sherwood had expected that it would take some 11 million pounds to achieve his objective, much of which has been spent to meet today's much more rigorous safety standards. The 17 Conti-nental and seven British carriages now used are truly magnificent, with the cost of restoration for once apparently no object.

The journey begins at Victoria Station in London, where passengers are seated in the most sumptuous first-class Pullman cars ever built, including one from the old Brighton Belle, which was, incidentally, the first Pullman train to operate in Europe. At Folkestone, reality returns rather abruptly in the shape of a Sealink ferry, also now owned by Sea Containers. For the moment, the most they can do is to ensure that Orient Express passengers are kept apart from the hoi polloi, in an exclusive verandah deck saloon, during the crossing to Boulogne.

At Boulogne's Gare Maritime, the original Orient Express cars stand alongside the plat-form in gold and dark blue livery, and their attendants, similarly dressed, wait by them. Luggage, collected in London and whisked unseen across the Channel, is deposited in the baggage car, and hand luggage placed in the compartments. They are luxurious, but scarcely spacious; as one of Hercule Poirot's suspects puts it, 'Come in gentlemen, if it's humanly possible'. It is, but the only sensible way to dress for dinner is in turns, one in, one out.

Dinner on the revived Orient Express

Once the train leaves, a pianist plays soft music on a grand piano to lure passengers to the bar, which did not exist on the original train – people had their drinks in the restaurant, or swigged away, silently, in their compartments. However, the Bar-Salon looks genuine enough, and the barman has an astonishing repertoire of cocktails. The pianist's repertoire is large, too.

After a few drinks, it is time for dinner, a prodigious gastronomic affair, served in three dining cars. There are at least seven courses, including caviare and smoked salmon, with vintage wines on offer. It is, quite simply, the best meal served on a train since the Second World War, and perhaps even before that.

By the time the train reaches Paris, the beds will have been made up in the compartments, which by night look stunning, with soft lamps, monogrammed sheets, and thick bath towels. Most passengers stay up, longer than is good for them, drinking the night away in the bar, where the indefatigable pianist is always the last to go to bed.

At dawn, with only the sleeping-car attendants still awake for the passport check, the Swiss customs officers arrive discreetly; the fresh croissants are taken on at Basle.

The Orient Express has given up the 12-mile spiral of the Simplon pass in favour of a more scenic route stopping at Zurich, St Anton and Innsbruck, with a winter detour to Landquart and Chur. Brunch follows breakfast before the train arrives finally at Venice, where the transport becomes gondolas and motor boats.

To enjoy the Orient Express, you have to enter into the spirit, dressing in thirties style, with haute couture for dinner. Only the spoilsports don't. Meals are included in the price (buttonhole the maitre d' to make sure of a first sitting for dinner, as the second is very late) but other than on the ferry crossing, drinks are extra, and can add as much as 15 per cent to the cost of your ticket, unless you are particularly abstemious. If you want to save money, take the train only as far as Paris, an 11-hour trip offered at a particularly favourable fare, to dove-tail with the passengers joining there. You will have dinner on board; the journey the following morning is frankly an anti-climax and so is the return journey, ending with the short trip from Folkestone to London, which has none of the romance or anticipation of arriving on the real Orient Express at Paris or Venice.

Gondola in a small canal, Venice

St Mark's on Ascension Day – Canaletto

Venice

If Venice is sinking gradually back into the sea, as the experts gloomily suggest, then it may be due to the sheer weight of tourists. There is no longer a best time to see the city, which offers a stark choice between the indifferent weather of the winter (which ruins the atmosphere) and the avalanche of visitors in the summer (which also ruins the atmosphere). The least unsatisfactory times to visit are, therefore, late April and May, or from mid-September to early October. June, July and August are quite disastrous: heat and hassle.

Even in the most agreeable months, the only way to appreciate the true beauty of Venice is to get up very early in the morning and walk around the narrow streets that crisscross the smaller canals. If you want to see any of the traditional sights, select one for each morning and be on the doorstep at 9am, when they usually open. These should certainly include the Doges' Palace, the symbol of Venetian power with its Grand Council Chamber; the Basilica, with its marvellous Byzantine mosaics and, in the Treasury, the spoils of the pillage of Constantinople; and the Academy of Fine Arts, a brilliant collection of paintings, including works by Titian and Bellini.

Unless you can afford the Cipriani (see below), staying in Venice itself is singularly unpleasant. It is noisy, hot and smelly. Even if you arrive on the Orient Express, when you simply walk down the station steps on to a motor launch on the Grand Canal, conveying luggage can be a problem. The answer is to stay on Venice Lido, an island with magnificent beaches opposite the city and, incidentally, a splendid view of Venice itself. Unlike the rest of Venice, the Lido actually has roads, and can be reached by an antiquated car ferry, which you join close to the huge car park at the entrance to the city.

HOTEL Cipriani

The only hotel in Venice with a swimming pool, and what a pool – easily Olympic size.

The owner, once again, is Sea Containers, on the reasonable premise that if you can afford the Orient Express, you can also afford the Cipriani. Strictly speaking, the Cipriani is not in Venice, but it is only three minutes by courtesy motor launch from St Mark's Square. The hotel is an elegant building on the island of Giudecca, out in the lagoon, the rooms and suites display impeccable taste, the fittings and furnishings are magnificent, and the food is as good, if not better, than anywhere in the city. Guess the cost, and then double it.

Grand Hotel des Bains

Dirk Bogarde's famous role as the ageing German besotted by a young boy in Visconti's *Death in Venice* was filmed in this hotel on the Lido. The des Bains may not be quite the luxury hotel of yesteryear, but its old-world charm remains. It has lovely rooms which face out to sea, overlooking miles of sandy beach and bathing huts; two swimming pools, one of them for toddlers, and a poolside restaurant offering delightful grills plus a restaurant of rare elegance and quality. A free launch service runs into Venice, ten minutes across the lagoon; and they will even meet you by boat at the airport. Compared to the Cipriani, the des Bains is positively cheap.

—————— MOTORAIL ——————

Most overnight railway journeys are for sado-masochists or insomniacs. There is, however, one glorious exception. Every day of the year, come rain or shine, heatwave or snowstorm, the longest rail journey in France can take you and your car to the Mediterranean and let you sleep on to a reasonable hour. This is the service from the Gare Maritime at Calais to Nice, $14\frac{1}{2}$ hours of travel and, if you are lucky, almost as many degrees Celsius difference in temperature.

There is a myth about motorail: that it is prohibitively expensive. It will certainly not be cheaper than cramming the family into the car and driving through the night from one end of France to the other on minor roads, but for anyone planning overnight stops and using motorways, it is a viable alternative. You save on hotel bills, additional meals and drinks, petrol, oil and motorway tolls. In the long run you also save on garage bills, through less wear and tear on the car. Even more important, you save an intangible amount of human wear and tear and allow the family to enjoy the holiday from the moment they arrive.

Motorail travel obviously begins by loading the car on to the transporter – which you can do yourself or let the French railwaymen do for you. Even an experienced motorailer may feel a qualm when his car disappears from view, particularly on the Calais-Nice service, where the transporter is shunted off to some siding to await the arrival of the train. The passengers, too, must wait as the sleeping compartments are part of a regular service.

There is, however, a $14\frac{1}{2}$ hours journey ahead, and although French Rail do a valiant job in providing cold meals and drinks, a de luxe picnic requires rather more preparation. The solution is to take a slightly earlier ferry from Dover, and dash into the centre of Calais to buy French cheese, bread, wine, fruit and some of those splendid pâtisseries calculated to demolish the most conscientious diet. Thus fortified, the only remaining problem for the rest of the evening will be how to smuggle your bag of refuse down the corridor so that it blends with official railway debris outside the attendant's little office.

Soon the attendant will have realised that you want him to provide only mineral water and wine glasses, and that you are, to all intents and purposes, running a cross between a delicatessen and a wine bar. If he has really won your confidence, you may actually not look too worried when he takes away all your tickets, including the return halves, without bothering to mention that you will get them back in the morning.

Although it is not really very late, the combination of alcohol and anxiety syndrome can have left you feeling tired, so you will probably go to bed ridiculously early, just in time, in fact, for the arrival at the Gare du Nord in Paris, where Murphy's law dictates that you will pull up alongside a Turkish labourers' stopping train to Ankara, and your wife scarcely in her nightie.

Thoroughly awake by now, you spend the next hour working out exactly where you are as the train winds its way round Paris on an obscure through line which gives tantalising glimpses of the Sacré Coeur and a river that could conceivably be the Seine. But by now you have reached the Gare de Lyon, ready to be tacked on to a proper train again, heading south to the Côte d'Azur. The route still takes a lot of following, because there are no rail maps in French carriages: they were removed during the first World War to keep spies and saboteurs from being sure that they were blowing the right thing up and have never reappeared.

The anticipation and the excitement wakes you up early in the morning, and you begin to regret that you have ordered hot chocolate an hour later than the family next door. Soon, just outside Marseille, you get your first glimpse of the Mediterranean, shimmering in the sunshine. The next hour and a half or so is a kaleidoscope of the Côte d'Azur: glimpses of rocky coves and little boats; bigger ones in endless marinas; luxury flats by the sea; long, sandy beaches with unclad ladies doing what,

from the train, is the briefest striptease in history. You count off the stations of the French Riviera, Toulon, St Raphaël, Cannes, Antibes until, finally, the train tiptoes into Nice. Utter chaos. Luggage has never heard of the old saying, what comes out, must go back in. Will the train simply go on, if we don't get off? Where's the sea? Where's the car? The attendant is calm personified, flourishing return tickets and the night's reckoning like confetti. But then for him, it's just another day.

Motorail fares from the Channel coast are largely constant, so there is little advantage in travelling off-peak, although booking several months in advance is more or less essential if you want to travel during school holidays. The ferry crossing can be included as part of the package, at a discounted rate, which is not affected by the date and time of travel. This is of particular advantage to owners of large cars compelled to travel at peak weekends. The service to Nice leaves Calais at around 7.30 pm, arriving in Nice just before 10 am the following day. Continental breakfast is included in the fare.

Nice

More English than the English, Nice has pebble beaches and a four-mile Promenade des Anglais. The big difference is the cost of having a swim or getting a tan, for the few public beaches are disagreeably crowded, and unfavourably situated. The choicest spots are owned by the hotels opposite the Promenade, and you can gauge the cost of an umbrella, lilo or deck chair from the opulence of the hotel – the Negresco beach, for example, requires a second mortgage, particularly if you eat lunch at their beach restaurant, excellent though it is.

Nice, sheltered by high hills overlooking its Bay of Angels, has a mild climate throughout the year, which is reflected in the lush vegetation of its immaculate parks. The most interesting quarter to visit is the Old Town, honeycombed with narrow, slightly threatening streets, full of the smells of African

Motorail to the Mediterranean

cooking. But if you have the choice of where to stay, try the . . .

HOTEL Mercure

No better example than this of how to spend half the money and have the same view as the Meridien Hotel next door, because the two are physically integrated, so much that the balcony above can be part of the 4-star luxury hotel. The Mercure has few public rooms, but travelwise guests have been known to use the emergency stairs and drop into the ground-floor Meridien bar. It is vital to stipulate a room with a sea view, because the others, overlooking a rear courtyard, are dingy and claustrophobic. The Mercure has its entrance in a side street off the Promenade des Anglais, and is ideally situated for the Place Massena, a pedestrian area of open-air restaurants and boutiques which never seem to close.

— LE TRAIN À GRAND — VITESSE

A train can never beat a plane, except, that is, when it is Le Train à Grand Vitesse. The Great Speed Train, to give the literal translation, is, for once, not an advertising hyperbole. It does travel at great speed for much of its journey and, judged on a city-centre to city-centre service, it can be faster than an aircraft over certain distances. Between Paris and Lyon, for example, the rail journey takes two hours exactly: by air, almost as long (and longer during the rush hours), counting travelling time to Orly and from Lyon airport into the centre. Small wonder that more than half the passengers who used to travel on this route by air, now go by rail. Even between Paris and Geneva, which now takes 3 hours 32 minutes by TGV, more than

Le Train à Grand Vitesse

15% of regular passengers have switched their allegiance to rail, preferring the convenience of the longer journey between the two city centres to the effort of getting taxis, hanging about at airports, plus the actual flight.

What has made this transformation possible (and which enhances the importance and prestige of the railways in this age of air travel) has been the construction of a new electrified track between Paris and Lyon, with a spur towards Dijon, on which the TGV can travel at speeds of up to 168 miles per hour. Unlike other fast rail systems, the train does not have to vary its speed to cope with bends and tunnels; the track has only the gentlest of curves and no tunnels or level crossings. The massive power-cars – too modern to be described as engines – can generate up to 6300kW, making it possible for the TGV to travel at more than 200mph on its special track although, for safety reasons, it never does. However, the additional power is not superfluous; it allows the TGV to thunder up and down gradients as though they did not exist.

Despite its huge power, which creates a crescendo of noise in the narrow passageway that links the driver's cabin to the rest of the train, the TGV is an extremely quiet train. Rather like Concorde, passengers sometimes have a twinge of disappointment, because the sensation of tremendous speed is simply not there. It is only when you look out of the window and see big Citroens and Mercedes, obviously moving at high speeds on motorways, reduced virtually to snails, that the rate at which you are travelling becomes apparent. Even the acceleration is barely noticeable, as the TGV can reach its highest permitted speed so smoothly in a matter of minutes.

You will never be seated immediately over the wheels, because they are all placed between the carriages. The special rolling stock always consists of eight carriages with a power car at each end, although two sets can be run coupled together. The seats are similar to those in aircraft, though with more leg room, and with folding tables for drinks or papers. Every carriage has a number of facing seats for groups of four people. In first class, there is a double row of seats on one side of the aisle and a single row by the window on the other; in second class, there is a double row of seats on either side of the aisle.

No-one is allowed to stand on a TGV, so passengers need both a ticket and a seat reservation. Unlike other rail systems, this need does not involve queuing at a booking office because the TGV ticket system is fully computerised. On the principal stations serving the TGV network, a machine enables you to make reservations on the first TGV with seats available that is leaving in the next $1\frac{1}{2}$ hours. It can accept instructions for first or second class, whether in first class you wish to take up the option (up to one hour before departure) of having a hot meal brought to your seat during the journey, and whether or not you are prepared to pay a supplement for travelling on certain departures during peak hours. You can even buy a book of supplement coupons in advance and use them whenever the need arises.

In first class, the hot meals include the choice of a grill or the day's 'special'. In second class, a trolley service of cold dishes is served at your seat. If you do not want a full meal, a buffet in the centre of the train offers sandwiches, drinks, even newspapers and cigarettes. It is, however, frequently crowded, the one aspect of the TGV that needs improvement. When the special eight-carriage sets come up for renovation or replacement, French Railways intend to enlarge the buffet cars considerably.

The TGV is the first train to cater for handicapped passengers and for children travelling on their own. Wheelchairs can be accommodated in one of the first-class carriages, and for the price of a second-class ticket. On certain trains during the school holidays, children between 4 and 13 can be looked after by special hostesses for the whole of the journey.

On the TGV, you can travel the whole length of France between Lille and Toulon,

and without changing in Paris, which saves both time and considerable inconvenience. The journey time is only 4 hours 40 minutes. The TGV already serves much of south-east France as well as Geneva and Berne. and construction is under way on a new line to the south-west which will reduce journey times on the route to Bordeaux. The Great Speed Train is here to stay.

For tourists, by far the most interesting section of the TGV is between Paris (Gare de Lyon) and Lyon, which has a special station for TGV services, as most of the track on this route has been specially constructed; it is on this route that the train travels at its top speed.

Lyon

One of the largest cities in France, Lyon originally owed much of its prosperity to a monopoly in the silk trade, and it still keeps its international trading connection by playing host to a number of fairs. Situated at the meeting point of the Rhône and the Saône, its old city on the hill has a remarkable collection of Renaissance and medieval buildings, including a great cathedral. Lyon's principal claim to fame in modern times is as a centre of gastronomy, having a collection of some of the finest restaurants in all France. One of the oldest is the Kléber Restaurant in the Place Kléber, where the owner, Pierre Orsi, is also its master chef. The Kléber is not as outrageously expensive as some of its competitors. If you intend to spend a few hours in Lyon, they are better employed eating rather than sight-seeing, unless you have time to travel some 20 miles north-west to:

Pérouges

A perfectly preserved medieval village with timbered houses, narrow cobbled streets, and a 15th-century manor house which forms part of the Ostellerie du Vieux Pérouges, run by the Thibaut family. Here you will find superb food, and a wonderful period atmosphere.

Bullet Train passing Mount Fuji

—— THE BULLET TRAIN ——

An American, whose watch looked capable of a moon launch, announced to anyone who was listening that the Bullet Train had left Tokyo eight seconds late. The other tourists pretended to ignore him, but a Japanese railway official who understood English was stung into explanation. 'The train is on time', he declared. 'The train leaves eight seconds after the doors close, to allow last arriving passenger time to sit down.'

It is a measure of Japanese precision that their train services are monitored in seconds, rather than minutes, and that you can, indeed, set your watch by the Shinkansen express, the Bullet Train, which links all the major cities in Japan. Shinkansen means 'new trunk line' in Japanese, and although the last link in the chain between Ueno and Omiya north of Tokyo was opened only in 1985, the Bullet Train concept is now far from new. The very first Shinkansen service began in October 1964, when a train travelling over long distances at 130mph was indeed revolutionary. Now, of course, it is little faster than the British HST 125, and considerably slower than the French 168 mph TGV.

What the Shinkansen *does* offer is still unique – a service of express trains, on a welded rail system, which is completely separate from the standard network. In contrast, British High Speed Trains run on the same rails as slower services, and the French TGV, though boosted by sections of special track, begins and ends its journey on the same lines as other trains. Only the Shinkansen is completely separate, with a signalling system so sophisticated that nine trains each hour can run on the extremely busy section between Tokyo and the ancient capital of Kyoto, separated by only a few minutes despite their speed. Although the trains do have drivers, they are usually controlled automatically and are linked to a computer-aided traffic control system.

A little like Concorde, the speed at which you are travelling is displayed, in the Shinkansen's case, in a corner of the buffet. Here, too, is a telephone linked into the full Japanese network, by no means extraordinary nowadays, but once well ahead of its time.

The Shinkansen is not quite perfect. Because the journey times are so fast – three hours, for example, on the 320 mile journey between Tokyo and Kyoto – meals are less vital and frankly leave a good deal to be desired. The seats, even in first class, are not exceptionally comfortable, with insufficient leg room for taller European visitors. Even the amazing automatic traffic system has been known to fail occasionally, the victim of an unforeseen phenomenon. In colder weather, the warm computer boxes are a tempting place of refuge for cockroaches, and when they scamper around inside, some very strange signals can close down the Shinkansen completely.

Tokyo

As most people arrive in Japan at the end of a demanding flight, Tokyo's international airport, Narita, can be a harrowing experience. Immigration alone can take an hour or more, because the Japanese take form-filling and form-reading seriously, and have preferential queuing only for their own citizens. Unlike many other airports, therefore, it is certain that your luggage will arrive at the top of the conveyor belt long before you do. Narita is also 35 miles from the centre of Tokyo, a journey which in the rush hours can take at least two hours, and possibly considerably longer. Steel yourself, therefore, to not reaching your hotel room until three hours after touch-down. If you are not on an inclusive tour, and therefore provided with transport into the city, note that taxis are extremely expensive and unlikely to be any faster than the orange Limousine buses, which go to the Tokyo City Air Terminal or TCAT for short, situated near the Ginza shopping centre. The main hotels are also served by special buses.

Car hire is quite possible at Narita, and the Japanese drive on the left with right-hand steering wheels (there are some countries with *left*-hand drive cars that have to be driven on the left as well), so this should make the task simpler; however, be warned that virtually none of the road signs in Tokyo is displayed in English. Once you are lost, you stay lost, so equip yourself with a detailed street map. Strange though it may seem, the 'Skyliner' train into Tokyo, run by a private company, runs only as far as the northern suburb of Ueno because of environmental disputes. There are plans to link the airport, by rail, to Tokyo's main station but this is a long way from completion.

Getting around

As joining a crocodile line of tourists wears thin very rapidly, finding your own way about Tokyo is a priority. Most taxi drivers do not speak a word of English or understand anything written in English, so the most essential item to carry is a card, written in Japanese, bearing the name of your own hotel. If you can obtain a similar card for your intended destination, so much the better, otherwise get someone at your hotel to write it out in Japanese. Even then, do not assume that the taxi driver is likely to know the way; many seem to have only a rudimentary knowledge of the city, so marking where you are going on a map can have distinct advantages. However because the traffic in Tokyo seems to be at a permanent standstill for much of the day, by far the most efficient way to get about is on the Tokyo Underground, whose station signs are displayed in English. The system runs on colour-coded lines, with trains in matching colours, so it is extremely difficult to lose your way. During the morning and evening rush hours, the Underground is incredibly crowded, so much so that a train in the equivalent period in London would be thought by the Japanese to be almost empty. The experience is unimaginably worse during the winter months, when the volume of each passenger is increased by his or her overcoat, and when the railway employs pushers and shovers to get everyone in.

Shopping

Tokyo is a city for innovations, not bargains. If you want the very latest in electronic or photographic goods, Tokyo is bound to have them available – but at a price. Anything which has been on sale for a year or more will have arrived in Europe and will be much cheaper in London. If, however, you are determined to return with some piece of electronic wizardry, take a notebook to the Ginza rather than your money, and write down the prices (and the exact model numbers) of promising items in the department stores, which open at 10 am and close at 6 pm. Then find your way to the Akihabara market (for electronic goods) or the My City shopping complex in Shinjuku (for camera equipment), where the prices are lower and, with determined bargaining, can be reduced still further. For Japanese prints, try the little shops in the Kanda district; if you are looking for genuine antiques, and are not an expert, it is extremely difficult to be certain of what you are buying.

Touring Japan

The key is not to try to do too much. After Tokyo and its inevitable city tour, Kyoto, Nara and Himeji have perhaps the most to offer. The furthest is Himeji, though served by the Shinkansen to the west beyond Kyoto, with its spectacular 'Heron Castle', a 14th-century feudal castle of great beauty with gleaming white walls. Nara, capital of Japan in the eighth century, can be reached by rail though not by the Bullet Train; it is south of Kyoto, where you have to change. Nara has the Todaiji Temple, where Buddhism flourished under the patronage of the Emperors, it has a stupendous Buddha image; and the Horyuji Temple, erected early in the seventh century, making it the oldest surviving wooden structure in the world. But Kyoto, formerly the capital of Japan, has its own fascinating wooden building, Ninomaru Palace, with its whispering floor, deliberately designed to creak at the slightest touch – the means by which the military ruler of Japan, the Tokugawa Shogun, made it impossible for even the invisible assassins of the Ninja to approach him unheard. The rest of Kyoto, with its Old Imperial Palace, its exquisite gardens and traditional way of life, is a marvellous experience. If the weather is clear, the snow-capped peak of Mount Fuji, the highest mountain in Japan, will be visible

Castle at Himeji

from the Shinkansen between Kyoto and Tokyo.

Japanese Railways offer a rail pass for unlimited travel to visitors, which can be collected on arrival at Narita Airport or at Tokyo Central Station (on production of your passport), but which must be paid for in advance in the UK.

HOTELS

Century Hyatt

One of the newest, and finest, hotels in Tokyo, with larger and more comfortable bedrooms than most, 800 in all on 28 floors. Take the lift to the top for the huge Sky Pool—Olympic lengths and Olympian views. On the way up, marvel at the three huge, spectacular chandeliers that tower over a foyer the size of a railway station but much, much more elegant. The hotel's 12 restaurants include the Chenonceaux, with French cuisine which would not be out of place in the best establishments in Paris. The Century Hyatt has its own direct coach service from the airport and runs a shuttle service every few minutes to the nearby Shinjuku shopping centre, where the Odakyu Department Store offers a ten per cent discount for Hyatt guests.

New Otani

Not so much a hotel, more a town, a vast edifice consisting of the original construction plus a huge new tower, which is at least half a mile from the front desk. On the way there, however, you pass by the Otani's pièce de résistance, a 400-year-old Japanese garden, complete with waterfalls, bridges and pagodas, and considering the number of people in the hotel at any one time, practically deserted. As this is the largest hotel in Asia and, by Japanese standards, most reasonably priced, the lobby sometimes seems like an extension of the subway in rush hour. However, it is admirably run and the food, especially in the French Restaurant, La Tour d'Argent, is uniformly excellent. The rooms, are, however, decidedly poky, especially in the new tower. Below stairs lies a different town altogether, for the staff, with another set of restaurants and shops. And, who knows, perhaps another below that for the people who look after them. . .

— MEXICO —

The train to Texas

The train traveller in Mexico must be alert to the system's eccentricities. Although there is a vast network of lines, not all of them are in good condition and many journeys, which might be supposed to take hours, in fact take days. As a result, Mexican Railways offer sleeper services on a good many routes, and the schedules are designed to include much overnight travel. One of the best routes to see the real Mexico, rugged terrain, poor villages, and positively no tourists, is the line that winds its way from Mexico City through Leon to San Antonio in Texas, once of course part of the Mexican Empire. A brief stop in Leon can be quite rewarding, because this is real commanchero country, with a railway station where the livestock always outnumber the human passengers, some of whom still have horses, spurs and an assortment of weapons that would not be out of place in a museum. However, if you book to Leon, be sure that you have a berth in the one coach that stays there – it is uncoupled before dawn, and left on the main line, safe enough, because the next train does not arrive until the following day. Booking a berth in the wrong coach means, as one German businessman discovered to his cost, being unceremoniously put out on the platform in the middle of the night, the train then rumbling on. Even the correct coach has its hazards, as there is no attendant to wake you with coffee and biscuits. The first indication you will have that you may have overslept could be the jolt of the coach being coupled to a tank engine and taken off to some remote siding out of town.

Mexican sleeper compartments do have one advantage over their European counterparts: each has its own toilet. However, in order to use the toilet in the single compartment, the occupant has to fold his or her bed back into the wall, a task roughly as complicated as assembling a tent in a gale. Should you be struck down with Montezuma's Revenge, you would therefore be in for an exhausting night. The solution is relatively simple: Mexican trains are so cheap that you could seriously consider buying two train and two sleeper tickets and having a much less cramped double compartment all to yourself.

The Alamo, San Antonio

Teotihuacan, Pyramid of the Sun

While the Romans still occupied Britain, south of Hadrian's Wall, the great civilisations of Central America were building their temples to the gods, whose massive ruins survive – including at Teotihuacan, 30 miles north of Mexico City, the most important archaeological site on the Continent: the Pyramids of the Sun and the Moon, as large as the great Pyramids of Egypt. Further south, near Oaxaca, is the extraordinary Monte Alban, a plateau containing the religious city of the Zapotecs, largely intact because the conquistadores, unknowingly, passed it by. For a holiday which combines ruined temples with fabulous beaches, there is no place better than the Yucatán Peninsula, which has the Gulf of Mexico on one side and the Caribbean on the other, and with sites of the Mayan civilisation overlooking coral reefs and crystal blue waters. Acapulco has beautiful beaches, dominated by luxury hotels, but is frankly a disappointment – over-commercial, over-populated and over-priced. Most of the people back home will not know that, so for those who like sending postcards, it offers an unrivalled opportunity for one-upmanship.

Nearly half the inhabitants of San Antonio are of Mexican ancestry, and it was here that the Texas revolt against Mexican rule began in 1835, only to suffer a temporary setback at the siege of the Alamo the following year. This was an extraordinary siege in which 180 Texans held out against an army of 5,000 Mexican troops for 12 days and died to the last man. The defenders were led by Colonel James Bowie, inventor of the famous Bowie knife, and included the former Congressman David Crockett, private. The ruins of the Alamo, originally a mission church, are still preserved.

HOTEL Camino Real

No casual visitors here, except perhaps by private yacht, for the hotel is on the island of Cancun (whose name means 'pot of gold') off the Caribbean coast of the Yucatán Peninsula. It is a paradise for diving enthusiasts, with lovely warm water, and still largely unspoilt. The Camino Real, on the tip of the island, is luxurious but orientated towards the American market.

—— PALACE ON WHEELS ——

What James Sherwood and private enterprise has done for railway restoration and nostalgia in Europe, the public corporation of Indian Railways has matched, carriage for carriage. Like Sea Containers, they set out to recreate a style of travel long departed and almost forgotten. The result is the 'Palace on Wheels', relics of a bygone age when the British still pretended that India was ruled by the princes.

The princes may have been deprived of real power but they did not lack for wealth and the trappings of authority. These railway coaches were their playthings, the Indian equivalent of Mr Toad's car. They were not allowed to own engines or to drive trains after a series of accidents in the last century in which Maharajahs had simply concluded that red signals did not apply to them. If they wanted to go anywhere, they had to ask the railway companies to provide an engine.

So the princes put their creative energy into their carriages, which subsequently had to be tracked down throughout the length and breadth of India and Pakistan. One or two had been wrecked, victims of the inevitable crashes and collisions through the years, which were a feature of the railways when the British used to run them but which have happily been much reduced. Some coaches had come to rest at the side of the track, where they were often being used to house some cottage industry, the squatters blissfully unaware of their origins. Other coaches, more shrewdly, were being used as unofficial railway offices, parked in sidings at obscure stations, and sometimes accommodating a junior station master's entire family. All of these exotic carriages had been stripped of their fine furnishings and were rusting away in the monsoon rains.

A dozen or so coaches were eventually recovered and painstakingly restored. The oldest, and most famous, coach was once owned by the Maharajah of Bikaner, and ran on the Jaipur Railway. Nowadays you have to make do with two servants where the Maharajah would probably have had seven or eight. They call themselves coach captains, and dress, complete with turban, in traditional attire. One of them serves snacks and drinks in the coach sitting room, roughly the equivalent space occupied by 48 first-class passengers on British Rail, but furnished rather better with settees and armchairs, covered in the plushest of pink velvet upholstery. The other coach captain busies himself in either the bedroom or the bathroom, for the 'Palace on Wheels' has both, with enough room to make the overnight sleeper to Inverness seem like a tin coffin. In the bedroom, the bed and the panelling are in matching teak, the bed with a brocade headboard, and wide enough for two. The curtains have been perfectly matched to the originals, with embroidery in real silver, and there cannot be a plusher train carpet anywhere in the world.

Each coach is an entity in itself because none of them has a corridor. When the princes were travelling and their coaches offered unimaginable luxury in comparison with the cattle-truck conditions of the remainder of the train, there was no conceivable reason why they would have wanted to wander down a corridor to discover how the other half travelled. Still less, would they have been desirous of unwelcome visitors obtaining access to their coach; without corridors, they could remain cocooned in their own little world.

The traveller on today's 'Palace on Wheels' must, therefore, alight from his private coach when the train stops, in order to visit the rest of the carriages. These include a restaurant car which bears an uncanny resemblance to the new Orient Express, which is not surprising when one remembers that in the days of the Raj, its workmanship was probably the creation of the same craftsmen in Derby or some such point north. The European food, it must be said, is not up to the Orient Express, though the Indian dishes are magnificent.

The 'Palace on Wheels' runs anti-clockwise in a triangle from Delhi through the desert state of Rajasthan; dinner, bed and breakfast are usually offered on the train, before the traveller steps off for a day's hectic sight-seeing. The welcome at each station is a little disconcerting, as successive station masters vie with one another to achieve the most spectacular greeting. Massed pipe bands of the Indian Army and a row of trumpeting elephants can, occasionally, be

Bedroom of the Palace on Wheels

too much of a good thing just after breakfast. Especially if you have been deprived of sound sleep by the violent rocking of the train as it passed over one of the many joins, perhaps better described as gaps, in the track. The continuous welded rail has yet to reach the Indian railway network in any significant proportion. The one compensation is that the large number of unscheduled stops for one reason or another does enable the traveller on a corridorless train to visit the bar and his fellow passengers at regular intervals without the risk of being stranded for the night away from his luxurious bed – although the commodious sofas in the other coaches are a perfectly acceptable alternative.

Where the 'Palace on Wheels' scores so heavily over the Orient Express is in its means of propulsion. Try as they did, Sea Containers were never able to discover the hardware or the route in Europe that would have enabled them to revive the Orient Express exactly as it once was – a steam train. In India this presents no problem, because more than half the locomotives are still driven by steam, and take on water at remote, unheard-of halts, from sinister-looking tanks that one half expects any moment to disgorge an ambush of warrior Rajputs. The engines used on this particular run are, indeed, something special to fit the occasion, prodigies of gleaming brasswork, lovingly polished by Indian crews for whom they are the Concordes of the tracks, and the pinnacle of their profession.

If you compliment them on the turn-out of the locomotive, more often than not the 'Fort of Jodhpur', they will invite you on to the footplate to sample the noise and the sweat, the smut and the steam for yourself. Shovel in a little fuel, and you just might be awarded the ultimate accolade, and be allowed to handle the controls for a minute or two on a clear, straight run. To be in charge of the 'Palace on Wheels', even for a fleeting moment, at the gateway to Agra, home of the Taj Mahal, is a rare privilege; enough to revive that schoolboy determination to be an engine driver when, or if, one grew up.

INDIA'S FORTS AND MEMORIALS

Delhi

The grand design of the Moghul Emperors and the extravagant follies of the Maharajahs made India what it is, an unrivalled mixture of power and impotence, of civilisation and cruelty, of epic construction and squalid poverty. But the contradictions are part of its charm, ensuring that even a brief visit to this vast sub-continent, more than 2,000 miles from north to south, is an unforgettable experience.

When the Moghuls came to India early in the 16th century, Delhi, for a time, was their capital. The Moghuls transformed northern India into a land of sandstone forts which sheltered the far pavilions of gleaming marble, each adorned with gold and jewels on an unimaginable scale. Palaces, mosques and, above all, tombs and monuments, rose into the sky, the product of ceaseless toil by India's teeming millions. In Delhi, many of their amazing works survive – the Red Fort, with its huge ramparts and exquisite palaces; the imposing minaret of Qutb Minar; Jama Masjid, the largest mosque in India; and the Tomb of Humayun, the first of the great Moghul Emperors. The Moghuls left more than mere bricks and mortar: in essence, they created a climate which enabled India, perhaps unknowingly, to accept British rule and then the regime of Mahatma Gandhi without losing its true sense of purpose. Delhi has elements of all, fine gardens and avenues created by the British as though it were Kent or Surrey, and the Raj Ghat, where the body of Gandhi burned on its funeral pyre.

HOTEL Taj Mahal

Of the many fine hotels in Delhi, this has strong claims to be the best; it is modern, air-conditioned and situated in one of the most pleasing parts of the city. It has five restaurants, one beside the magnificent swimming pool, and incredible service. For a visitor determined to do Delhi until he drops, there is no better place to stage a recovery.

Humayun's Tomb, Delhi

Jaipur

Capital of the rugged desert kingdom of Rajasthan, Jaipur is where the Maharajah Jai Singh constructed not just a palace, but almost an entire city, in rose-pink stone. He was obsessed with astronomy, and added, in 1728, the Jantar Mantar observatory. The women of his household, deprived of outside contact, had their own vantage point to look down on the bustling life of the city below, the fabulous Palace of the Winds.

HOTEL Rambagh Palace

An incredible former royal residence built in 1727, set in superb, landscaped gardens, with an indoor marble swimming pool. Its famous Polo Bar has memories of the heyday of the Raj when the sahibs relaxed over gin fizzes as the sun went down.

Jodhpur

The rugged desert spawned a race of equally rugged warriors, the Rajputs, whose buildings were designed for security and defence, but were no less magnificent in their construction than other palaces. At Jodhpur, standing on the edge of the Thar Desert, the skyline is dominated by the massive Meherangarh Fort, founded in 1459 by the Rajputs, and now the home of an extraordinary collection showing Indian culture through the centuries.

HOTEL Umaid Bhawan Palace

Once the home of the Maharajah Umaid Singh, the Palace has been turned into a superb hotel with full air-conditioning, an indoor swimming pool and two outstanding restaurants.

Palace of the Winds, Jaipur

Agra

The Moghuls prepared for the next world in a way which guaranteed their earthly immortality, a paradox that produced the most awe-inspiring mausoleum of all, the Taj Mahal. A building of such exquisite symmetry, such unrivalled grandeur, could only have been created by someone inspired . . . and the inspiration was grief. Shah Jehan felt the loss of his wife, Mumtaz, so deeply that he devised a memorial so vast that it took 20,000 workmen, some of them brought from the Renaissance centres of Italy, 21 years to complete.

The Taj Mahal should be visited at least twice, once at sunset, an experience that stirs the senses, and once in the strong, clear light of day, to touch the cool white marble and marvel at the devotion of Shah Jehan, whose own much smaller tomb lies alongside that of the wife he loved so much. The tomb of Mumtaz bears an inscription placed by the grief-stricken Shah: 'Help us, O God, to bear that which we cannot bear.'

CHAPTER 3

HOLIDAY CHOICE

──── COSTA BRAVA ────

Rugged country, dramatic views and a coastal road that winds in and out of bays, offering tantalising glimpses of hidden coves below: this is the real image of the Costa Brava – a far cry from the popular concept of a Spain catering only for mass tourism. With an increasing number of flight-only deals available, and Gerona Airport within easy reach, intending visitors are no longer restricted to the traditional package tour resorts and hotels, epitomised by Lloret de Mar.

Cadaqués

Lloret is in the southernmost part of the Costa Brava. For a true taste of Spain, go north, then east, on to the Peninsula of Cabo de Creus, where the foothills of the Pyrénées run down to the sea. This is a sparse, desolate area, making the first sign of life all the more dramatic. Rising out of the sky are the dazzling white houses of Cadaqués, red roofs gleaming in the sun, a fishing village so picturesque that it is a magnet for artists, whose easels clutter up the quaint little quaysides. The great surrealist painter, Salvador Dali, was so entranced with the place that he bought a tiny fisherman's cottage just along the coast. Officially, fishing (though more probably smuggling) remains a minor activity in the village, though some of the fishermen make more money towing water skiers around the bay. Cadaqués, an ancient town with a Greek and Roman past, has a chequered history. It was a tempting target for marauding bands of corsairs, one of whom,

Cadaqués

led by the formidable and ferocious Barbarossa, sacked the village in 1543, burning the church and many of the nearby houses. Nowadays, the only invaders come in motor cars, making the drive along the peninsula frustratingly slow in summer.

Rosas

On the southern tip of the Cabo peninsula, Rosas offers a superb stretch of gently sloping sandy beaches, set against the dramatic backcloth of the Pyrénées. Once it was more than simply a seaside resort: the base of the formidable Catalonian navy; now all that remains is the fishing fleet. Shopping in Rosas is a positive pleasure, because the main streets are permanently closed to traffic. But the calm is deceptive, as Rosas has a flourishing night life, including two nearby casinos, one of them in a 16th-century castle at Perelada. Also close by, and not to be missed, is the remarkable Castelló de Ampurias, a medieval walled town with cobbled streets and a lavish church, reminders of its heyday before it was left stranded by the sea. A little further south are the ruins of Ampurias itself, with traces of Phoenican traders who founded it, the Greeks and the Romans – Caesar settled some of his veterans here.

HOTELS

For comfort and entertainment, the marina complex of hotels and apartments at Ampuriabrava, five miles to the south of Rosas, will appeal to many. Although designed for boating enthusiasts, it has every conceivable outdoor activity, without many of the disadvantages usually associated with a holiday centre.

Estartit

Of all the major Costa Brava resorts, Estartit remains the most genuinely Spanish, making fewer concessions to the huge influx of tourists each summer. Aficionados of sand castles declare that the Estartit sand has exactly the right texture for their construction – although locally produced beach spades are not as child-resistant as those made in the UK. If sun bathing ceases to appeal, boat trips are available to the offshore Medas Islands, once a pirates' lair. Many holiday-makers ask whether it is worth the transfer time from Gerona – double the 40 minutes to Lloret de Mar. It is.

HOTEL Miramar

If you hate a long walk to the beach, the Miramar is ideal, as it is a mere two minutes away. But it has its own shaded gardens should the sun become too hot, and two swimming pools, including one for children. The best rooms are on the second floor.

Aiguablava

An exquisite little cove, perfectly sheltered even on the windiest of days, and almost completely unspoilt. Accessible only from the sea is the Cueva d'en Gispert, named after the man who discovered it, a remarkable cave that winds for hundreds of yards into the cliffs. Local fishermen have the unofficial franchise to take you there: fierce bargaining is called for.

HOTEL Parador Costa Brava

Above Aiguablava is the only parador, or state-run inn, on the Costa Brava, built into the cliffs and affording superb views out to sea. As, like all paradors, it is not planned primarily to operate at a profit, it offers remarkable value in high season; not surprisingly, then, booking many months in advance is absolutely essential.

Palamós

No fish can be fresher than at Palamós, where hoteliers and residents alike turn up late in the afternoon at La Lonja, the auction rooms, to bid for the best of the fishing fleet's catch, spread out in trays on the floor. Boats and bathers intermingle on the broad sandy beach, so you may have to be careful to avoid getting oil on your clothes. But for those who like a quiet resort for a traditional seaside holiday, this is ideal.

S'Agaró

Two miles beyond the skyscraper hotels of Playa de Aro is the exclusive resort of S'Agaró, with luxurious villas set in delightful pine-shaded gardens overlooking the cliffs around the beach. A splendid promenade leads on to San Pol, one of the few beaches in Spain to charge admission.

HOTEL Hostal de la Gavina

Matching the resort, one of the most famous (and most expensive) hotels in the whole of Spain. The food is superb, the decor incredible, and the public rooms magnificent. All the suites have period furniture and bathrooms fit for a Roman emperor.

EXCURSIONS

Gerona
No fewer than 34 sieges of Gerona have taken their toll of the city walls, whose remnants are scattered around the circumference like some child's half-finished construction kit. They enclose the fascinating old quarter, a muddle of tiny streets and steps, bridges and passageways, where small family businesses are conducted much as they were centuries ago. The Carrera de la Forfa has the pick of the antique and antiquarian book shops. It leads to the gothic Cathedral, whose matchless cloisters are overshadowed by an 11th-century tower, relic of an earlier cathedral. The cafés along the River Oñar provide both a respite and a sense of period atmosphere.

Barcelona
Spain's second city, but easily the most prosperous, with La Rambla, its five grand boulevards, offering every conceivable luxury and a taste of the richly varied society which flourishes under Barcelona's banner. Nearby, close to the Cathedral, is the Barrio Gótico, with buildings of gothic splendour.

Barcelona Cathedral

COSTA BLANCA

The White Coast of Spain, nearly 150 miles of sunshine and sandy beaches, has Benidorm in its midst; any holidaymaker who has gone there in high season expecting peace ,and quiet should change his travel agent. But Benidorm is by no means the be all and end all of the Costa Blanca; not far away are resorts of considerable charm and character and, inland, wild and spectacular scenery.

Benidorm
In the fifties this was a quiet fishing village – until the invention of the package tour. Nowadays, in a good year Benidorm fills its staggering 17,000 bedrooms for the whole of the summer season. If only as a cosmopolitan curiosity, Benidorm has to be seen and believed; its discos are among the best in Europe, the backbone of a truly dynamic night life. Thirty years ago, the beaches had more pebbles than sand; it had to be imported from Morocco.

HOTEL Don Pancho
An extremely comfortable and spacious hotel with two swimming pools, one of them for children, and the beach just five minutes away. Impressive floor shows five nights a week during the season. But, despite its size, few of the rooms have a sea view.

Villajoyosa
Nearly 20 miles north of Alicante, a quiet coastal town with medieval ramparts and a fortified church built into the walls. Villajoyosa also has an interesting old fishing quarter at the end of a delightful promenade shaded by palm trees, with some agreeable beaches beyond.

HOTEL El Montiboli
Two miles from the town, overlooking the sea, a hotel built in a rich mixture of Moorish and Spanish styles, two swimming pools, a beach club, and an outstanding restaurant.

Benidorm in the early 1950s

. . . 30 years later

Javea

At the mid-point between Alicante and Valencia, Javea threatens to become another Benidorm, so rapid is its development; but for the moment it still has its attractions, including the old fortified quarter and an astonishing modern church, whose sweeping lines are designed like the hull of a ship.

HOTEL Parador Costa Blanca

For yacht owners or hirers, or simply hangers-on, an extraordinary harbour specially built alongside the hotel, so you can almost check in without going ashore (come to think of it, if you have a yacht, why are you going ashore?). As Paradors go, disappointingly modern, but the service is superb.

EXCURSIONS

Cueva de Canalobre

Literally the Cave of Candelabra, in the hills between Benidorm and Alicante close to the village of Busot. The stalactites have acquired a remarkable formation, as though placed on the Devil's dining table; unfortunately, the *son et lumière* which accompanies the visit is completely over the top.

Polop de la Marina

Inland from Beniform on a rugged road that passes through a succession of small valleys, the village of Polop is singularly picturesque. It sits on a mound encircled by vivid mountain scenery, flanked by fruit trees.

Guadalest

A fortress in the hills, 17 miles north-west of Benidorm, accessible only on foot through a narrow archway cut into the rock. At its peak is a white bell tower, where the alarm was sounded to warn of intruders; and a tiny cemetery so short of space that the tombs were stacked one on top of the other. Much of Guadalest is, however, a ruin; what force of arms failed to achieve, an earthquake, in 1774, managed more successfully, splitting the rock and wrecking the foundations.

COSTA DEL SOL

After Switzerland, Spain is the most mountainous country in Europe. Nowhere is this more apparent than on the Costa del Sol, a narrow strip of sandy beaches between the sea and the mountains, offering an exciting contrast between resorts catering for every tourist taste, and tiny villages hidden in the hills, where life goes on much as it did centuries ago. The entry point by air is Malaga and, like the Costa Brava, one stretch of coast to the west receives the great majority of the holiday traffic, where Torremolinos and Marbella reign supreme. But east of Malaga, the resorts still have an identity in no way dependant on the tourist trade, the great city of Granada is more easily accessible, and the mountains of the Sierra Nevada – the location of so many spaghetti (or should it be paella?) westerns – are an easy drive away.

Nerja

A delightful village, if too popular a tourist spot, with half a dozen excellent beaches, and an increasing number of hotels. On the shoreline is a prominent promenade shaded by palm trees and lapped by the sea, known as the Balcón de Europa: a somewhat grandiose description derived from its opening (if you can open a promenade) by King Alfonso XII, when the town council were a little carried away. The view it provides along the coast, though, is superb. Nerja's almost claustrophobic streets and white-washed houses – traditional measures against the fierce Spanish sun – add to its atmosphere. If you wonder where all the local inhabitants are, the answer is in their back gardens – the village is full of little secluded patios, built originally by the Moors.

Nerja is all the more attractive because of its proximity to the Nerja caves, two miles away near the village of Maro. Discovered in 1959 by some adventurous Spanish boys, these huge, spectacular caverns contained bones, weapons and paintings dating back more than 20,000 years. They are open in the summer from 9 am to dusk, with no break for lunch, and shorter periods in winter.

A little further out of Nerja, but on a different road into the mountains, is the village of Frigliana. Its perfectly preserved Moorish architecture is quite exceptional.

HOTEL Parador de Nerja

This state-run hotel, with panoramic views of the sea and the mountains, has its own private lift to the Burriana beach, probably Nerja's best, delightful gardens, a huge swimming pool, and an excellent restaurant. The rooms, all with private bath, provide outstanding value; but frankly, the poolside bar prices are extortionate.

Almuñecar

The Phoenicians, the Romans (who built an impressive aquaduct) and, later, the Moors, settled at Almuñecar, which remains decidedly off the well-beaten tourist track – probably because it is a two-hour drive from Malaga airport.

The beaches are good, though mainly pebble, and most are overlooked by a pleasing promenade, shaded by spreading palms. The town itself has extraordinary charm. The steep streets of the San Miguel quarter, all donkeys and dust, could be out of an Arabic film; the Moorish castle at the top shows signs of sporadic shelling through the centuries.

Marbella and Puerto Banus (see page 38)

Those planning more than a brief stay to see the beautiful people should know that all the superior hotels are located some miles out of town, making car hire essential for even the most modest excursion and that as all the action is outside, the town of Marbella itself is a noisy anti-climax.

EXCURSIONS

Ronda

In the mountains behind Marbella, lies a different kind of Ronda valley – a deep gorge spanned by the very old (despite its name) Puente Nuevo, linking the two halves of Ronda village. The view from below, on one of the tracks beneath the castle, shows to

Ronda

most effect Ronda's forbidding location, and why it remained effectively independent for centuries. Visitors were not exactly welcome: a good many of them were simply thrown over the 600 foot cliff which stretches down from the old Moorish quarter to the bottom of the forbidding Tajo ravine.

Cordoba

The irresistible attraction of Cordoba is the Mezquita, a mosque dating back to the eighth century, when the city was a Moorish stronghold. Supported by 850 jasper and marble columns, the dome is truly spectacular, a measure of the Moorish power and prosperity which enabled Cordoba to grow to a population little short of a million at its zenith. The city declined under Christian rule, but the great mosque survived, with a Christian altar in its centre. Perpetually cool, no matter how high the exterior temperature, the Mezquita inspires a strange feeling of mystical power.

Seville (see page 41)

Granada (see page 40)

Gibraltar

Spain's entry into the Common Market ended the long closure of Gibraltar's frontier, though not the controversy over its political future. Homesick British tourists will be in paradise here, with red pillar boxes and bobbies on the streets and shops full of proper marmalade and Cheddar cheese (those, that is, not offering duty-free liquor or electronic goods) and a scene of frenzied activity whenever a cruise ship comes in. The view from the top of the Rock is spectacular, across to Africa on a clear day, and the barbary apes lurk near the halfway house on the cable car.

Morocco

Whether from Gibraltar or one of the nearby Spanish ports, it is possible to visit Morocco by ferry or hydrofoil. The markets of Tangier and its casbah are a fascinating experience – bargain for everything and do not eat any-

thing, if you value your stomach. The Spanish enclave of Ceuta, whose Mount Hacho was said to be the African end of the Pillars of Hercules, is another duty-free port. The Palace of the Calif at Tetuán, a town honeycombed with narrow streets and not so narrow traders, is of particular interest to those prepared to venture further afield.

MAJORCA

Of the four principal Balearic islands in the western Mediterranean, Majorca, Ibiza, Minorca and Formentera, Majorca is the largest, the most interesting and the most popular. Although it has become synonymous with the huge package tour industry, Majorca has a great deal more to offer than simply sunshine and sandy beaches. It is an island of astonishing contrasts – rugged mountain ranges, lush fertile valleys, and tiny villages clinging to terraced vine-clad slopes where time seems to stand still – all reached by narrow, winding roads with a surprise around almost every corner.

Formentor

A peninsula in the furthest north-east of the island, with stunning views of mountains and the azure-blue sea below. Not a place to take your eyes off the road, as hair-pin bends follow one another in quick succession. The actual village of Formentor is disappointing, a kind of service annexe to the luxury hotel which dominates the peninsula:

HOTEL Formentor

Haunt of dukes and kings, real and pop, an elegant hotel with beautiful views of mountains and sea from its lavish bedrooms, set in a wooded hillside with gardens gently sloping to an exquisite, private beach below. If the pedaloes and water-skiing become too much, guests can retire to one of the swimming pools – naturally there are two. You are also spoilt for choice in the restaurant, which has an astonishing range of international cuisine. An ideal choice for people who want to stay put and for whom money is practically no object.

Puerto Pollensa

For the less wealthy, but still discriminating visitor, Puerto Pollensa demonstrates that it is possible to absorb a substantial influx of tourists and retain a town's character. For, despite the arrival of several large hotels beside the sea, the dominant feature remains its traditional Spanish architecture, with imposing villas and arcaded cafés. The surrounding countryside is a treasure trove for the ornithologist and ideal for walkers.

HOTEL Daina

Ideally situated close to the town and the beach, the Daina provides extremely comfortable rooms with exceptional views of the mountains and the sea. If, at first sight, its swimming pool across the road on the promenade above the beach is rather odd, most of the guests end by preferring it, as they can be in the sea one minute and in the swimming pool the next. Only the waiters, sprinting back and forth with urgently needed replenishments for the poolside bar, have any real reservations.

Deya

Near the western coast of Majorca, still unspoilt and largely undiscovered, Deya stands as a testament of man's endless battle against nature. The village, which is reached by a winding and sometimes disquietingly narrow road from the east of the island, sits precariously at the top of a tiny hillside. Its steep, cobbled streets and stone houses were put together by peasants with their bare hands centuries ago. Now it is more a colony of artists and writers, inspired, or so they hope, by the earlier arrival of Robert Graves, who made Deya his home and led a successful campaign to preserve its architectural character.

Just outside the village is the imposing Son Marroig, once the royal residence of the Austrian prince, Archduke Ludwig Salvator, whose lengthy tome on Majorca first put the island on the tourist track, so he has a good deal to answer for.

Deya

HOTEL Es Moli

Seclusion may be synonymous with frustration, but not at Deya's Es Moli, an outstanding hotel with such charm and kindness that guests lose all sense of time, able to while away the hours without a moment's thought. The rich, tropical gardens, bordering on a swimming pool that compensates with elegance what it lacks in size, sustain the sense of seclusion. For those who have withdrawal symptoms when deprived of the sea, a distant view from their bedrooms, the Es Moli mini-bus, driven by a retired rally driver, takes only ten minutes to reach the rather bizarre beach, made by man and evidently disowned by nature.

Banyalbufar

A cliff-top village with a remarkable series of cultivated terraces, hewn out of the hillside like a giant's staircase, and a hidden smugglers' cove below. No good looking for grapes, though, even the smugglers grow tomatoes.

HOTEL Mar y Vent

A tiny hotel, run by the same enthusiastic Spanish family since the turn of the century, facing the sea, with a splendid sun terrace and two swimming pools, one heart-shaped, and one for children. Very comfortable rooms.

Estellenchs

Another unspoilt village to the south of Banyalbufar, with little stone houses nestling in the foothills. Steep, narrow paths lead down to the sea and a series of almost deserted coves strung along this steep and rocky coast.

HOTEL Maristel

Exceptionally, the annexe is the better part in which to stay, as the rooms are more comfortable, with sun terraces overlooking a small swimming pool. The restaurant, in the original part of the hotel across the road, is patronised by locals, always a sign of good food. Exceptional value.

Orient

No beaches and very few tourists in this quiet inland village in a valley of orange trees dominated by the Puig Mayor mountain. The coast is half an hour's drive away, but you may not need it if you stay at:

HOTEL L'hermitage

A Spanish duke built it, and it retains much of its original charm, with splendidly furnished public rooms and high beamed ceilings. The hotel has a swimming pool, tennis courts, and a restaurant justly famous for its food.

Puerto de Soller

A dilapidated old train takes tourists all the way from Palma, passing sensational mountain scenery, to the town of Soller, a rambling, curious place accustomed to seeing visitors pass it by – which is exactly what they do, for from Soller the route is by narrow gauge tram, using cars which were once said to ride up and down the streets of San Francisco. The facts, however, are rather different, for it seems the trams first saw light of day in a Barcelona backstreet, copied by someone who had pinched the plans.

Puerto de Soller is not quite such a delightful place as it seems from a distance. Its enchanting bay, almost a lagoon, has a regular traffic jam of yachts and fishing boats at its narrow entrance and the town cannot really absorb the massive influx of tourists, who swarm like ants over the little beach at the height of the season. But when the sun goes down and the day-trippers trip back to Palma, a less frenetic life begins in the bustling waterfront cafés, and even the native Majorcans come out to play.

HOTEL Marbell

Owned by a couple of Bestards . . . Tony and Bartolo Bestard; by no means a plush hotel but located on a small beach which escapes most of the day visitors. Extremely good value.

Palma

The capital of Majorca, Palma has a huge influx of tourists during the summer months. Their sheer numbers threaten to swamp the city, which out of season has great charm, especially its old quarter. But in summer the tourists swarm like ants. To escape them, at a price, stay three miles outside at:

HOTEL Sheraton Son Vida

A 13th-century castle, with majestic public rooms, enormous tropical gardens, a full-size private golf course, and two swimming pools, one under cover. Great luxury, no expense spared, especially by the guests.

MINORCA

An island of great tranquillity with none of the bright lights of the other Balearic territories or of the Spanish mainland. The Romans gave Minorca (meaning the 'smaller') its name, with plodding Roman logic, to distinguish it from Majorca (the 'larger'). You can imagine the conversation in a Roman galley: 'Left-hand down a bit, O Valerius, that's Majorca, we want Minorca'. When the Romans no longer wanted it, nearly every seafaring power did: the poor Minorcans were Spanish then British then French then British then Spanish then British and then finally Spanish in the 18th century, which must have made life difficult, to say the least. The great attraction of Minorca was its deep-water harbour, certainly the best in the Mediterranean, at Mahon, the capital. During their 70 years occupation, the British used it a great deal, though, contrary to rumour, Nelson never came here, or at least his meticulously kept diary never mentioned it. Nowadays, Minorca is less in demand, receiving barely a tenth of the tourists who visit Majorca, which is just as well, because the island has few real amenities apart from its beautiful scenery and fine beaches. Just outside Mahon in the village of Villa Carlos there is, however, one hotel with constant reminders of its interesting history:

HOTEL del Almirante

The British governor, Lord Collingwood, once lived in great splendour in this Georgian residence, and it is still most elegantly furnished. The hotel rooms provide exceptional views around the bay towards Mahon, and there are others, less atmospheric, situated around an agreeable swimming pool. Eat out.

Santo Tomas

Miles and miles of sand to the south of the picturesque village of San Cristobal.

HOTEL Los Condores Sol

In three wings, set around a large swimming pool, with grounds which run on to the sandy beach. Ideal for children, who have their own paddling pool. The buffet lunch is enormous.

Cala de Santa Galdana

On the south coast of Minorca, a delightful bay with a safe sandy beach and pine trees on the hills behind. However, exhausting yourself on long swims or watersports or all-day walks seems the only answer to the evenings, because while the hotels make an attempt at providing night life, it is pretty tame stuff.

HOTEL Audax

The best hotel in the resort, ideally situated close to the sandy beach. Almost all the rooms have a fine view of the sea.

Fornells

A picturesque fishing village in a huge bay on the north coast, famous for its seafood, usually served up with mayonnaise sauce, said to have been invented by a Mahon innkeeper (hence, Mahon-sauce) to disguise the unpalatable taste of some rancid meat he was serving his guests. Further east, the coast is almost deserted, but to reach these unfrequented beaches you must be prepared for a considerable walk, as the road runs out, too.

Cuidadela

On the west coast of Minorca, and formerly its capital before naval strategy dictated a move to Mahon. Cuidadela is, however, much the more attractive, with a pleasing mixture of Spanish and Moorish architecture, white walls, red roofs and shaded arches. What business is done in Cuidadela, is done in its bustling cafés.

IBIZA

Ibiza is Spanish through accident of geography rather than by natural inclination. Its people have always been fiercely independent, with their own almost incomprehensible dialect, the product of centuries of unwelcome visitors. In the old town of Ibiza, known as Dalt Vila, seven sets of fortifications can still be seen, almost perfectly preserved, built to keep out everyone from the Carthaginians to the Barbary pirates. When Hannibal gave the Romans a fright in their own backyard, he had two secret weapons: his elephants, and a lead sling shot the size of a golf ball, which could pierce a Centurion's shield at 50 paces. These shots were made in Ibiza, which can, therefore, claim to be one of the earliest centres of an armaments industry.

Today, the principal industry is tourism. Ibiza Airport is the sixth busiest in the whole of Spain. Many visitors, predominantly the young, are attracted by the bright lights and the promise of a pulsating night life; yet it is perfectly possible to lose oneself in the little coves along the coast.

San Antonio

This is where the action is, day or night. In the daytime, troops of tourists take off, by ferry, for the superior beaches outside the rather murky waters of the bay. At night, the waterfront cafés are a babble of different tongues, and the discothèques in the narrow streets behind provide a stereophonic cacaphony into the small hours. Finding an ideal hotel is almost impossible: you can have bands or beaches on your doorstep, but definitely not both.

Puerto San Miguel

A sheltered bay with a narrow inlet, once a Moorish settlement but now one of the more sophisticated resorts on the island. Behind the still unobtrusive row of tourist hotels are rugged cliffs and pockets of pine trees, marking the dusty road back to the parent village of San Miguel itself. Two miles outside is the best hotel in Ibiza:

HOTEL La Hacienda

The lovely cave of Na Xamena is nearby, the countryside is superb, and this hotel lives up to its marvellous setting. Built in traditional Spanish style, with sweeping lines and high arches, it provides outstanding service with great charm. The Hacienda has three swimming pools, one indoor, one for children, and one high up on a spectacular terrace – a peculiar shape, though, so serious swimmers will not like it. That minor flaw apart, the Hacienda offers a splendid, relaxing holiday.

Cala Vedella

The smart set comes here, sleeping on overcrowded yachts or in overcrowded villas, to keep down the cost. The harbour fans out into a long, delightful cove which, despite the winding road from San Antonio, still attracts a great many day trippers.

FORMENTERA

Formentera island got its name from the Latin frumenteria, meaning wheat producer, for Roman grain ships called there; now the ships are full of tourists, an hour's run out of Ibiza. The views on the way are better than the sights on the island itself, which is barely ten miles in length and has little to see. It was abandoned in the Middle Ages, menaced by Barbary pirates, and was only slowly repopulated in the 17th century. However, the sandy beaches are superb, especially those in the remote parts of the island. Be warned: if you hire a car, try the steering and the brakes; the island's mechanic evidently left some time ago.

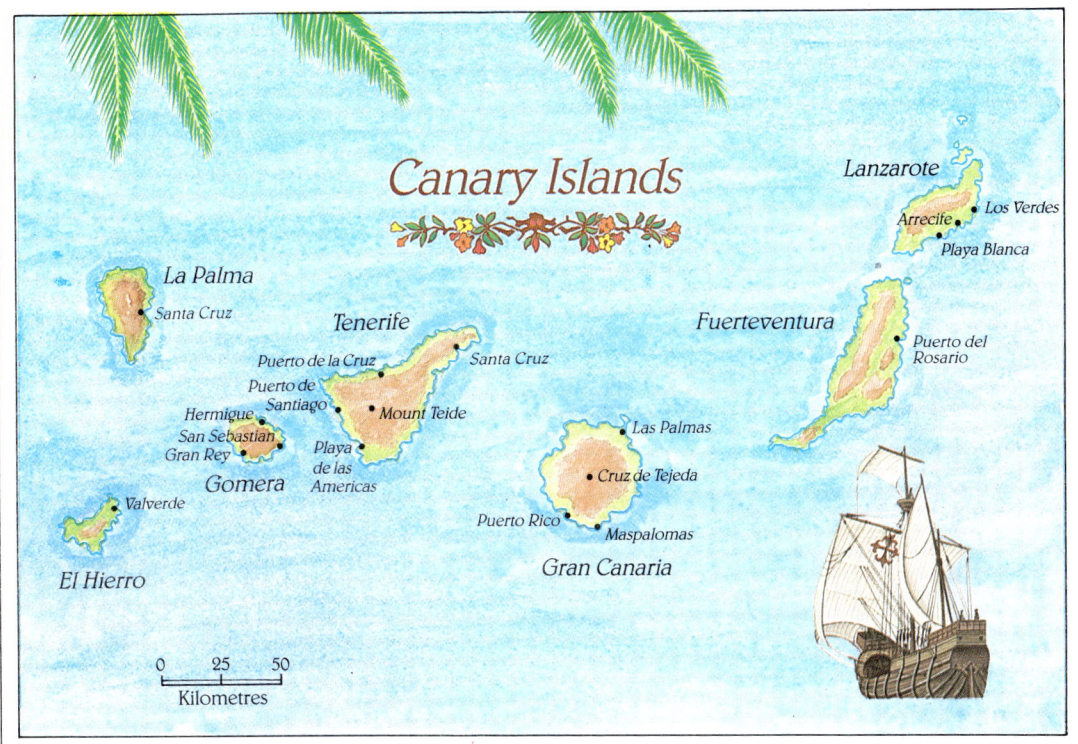

TENERIFE

Largest of the seven Canary Islands and the most frequented by tourists, Tenerife is dominated by a mountain, Teide, 12,195 feet above the sea. The long ridge below the peak divides the island in two, between the green, fertile north and the brown, barren south. It also divides the weather, because the north is cooler, cloudier and wetter. The south has most of the best beaches, and is much closer to the airport. It follows that Tenerife is one place where pinpointing your resort and your hotel is absolutely essential.

Puerto de la Cruz

The most visited resort in Tenerife, located in a sub-tropical valley; but it is one hour and a half by coach from the airport, adding a third more to your journey from the UK. Puerto de la Cruz also suffers from the major drawback of Tenerifean beaches – BLACK SAND, the product of its volcanic origins. It is no less comfortable to lie on, but psychologically it looks extremely uninviting. The town has tried to solve the problem by importing sand from Morocco by the million bucketfulls, and depositing it on the beach at Las Teresitas, just to the north. Unfortunately, this beach becomes extremely crowded at peak periods as does the lido in Puerto proper, a sequence of sea water pools. An hotel to which you can escape with conviction is, therefore, essential. A more temporary refuge. though no less agreeable for all that, are the Botanical Gardens, dating back to the 18th century. On view are orchid houses and a huge rubber plant.

HOTEL Botanico Sol

A long uphill walk from the town centre, should you bother, the hotel is situated in lovely scenery close to the Botanical Gardens. Two swimming pools, air-conditioned rooms, a night club (with extortionate bar prices), and a hotel restaurant as good as any in the island, which does not say a lot. Certainly the best hotel on Tenerife, if you can afford it.

HOTEL Tigaiga

A guide to the garden at the Tigaiga is provided, because it contains so many rare and exotic plants. The grounds are, indeed, beautiful, the kidney-shaped swimming pool surrounded by palm trees, the view in every direction superb. On fine Sundays, folk dancers perform on the terrace in front of the bar, and local chess players arrive looking for a game on the huge set in the garden. Comfortable rooms and realistic prices.

Playa de las Americas

More sunshine, much closer to the airport, and the sand isn't black . . . this time it's grey, almost as bad, with a beach that becomes extremely crowded in high season, and a sea frequently full of Atlantic rollers. So the choice of hotel is once again vital.

HOTEL Las Palmeras

Two swimming pools, including one for children, who are also provided with a playground. Extremely large, accommodating nearly 1,000 guests, but well run despite its size. Close to the centre.

Puerto de Santiago

On the sunny west coast, a much more restful resort, but unlikely to be for long, as apartments are going up fast. The scenery is superb, with dramatic cliffs called Los Gigantes – the Giants – without which one might assume that a Hotel called Los Gigantes was a joke from a Carry On film. But the sandy beach . . . yes, it's black.

HOTEL Los Gigantes Sol

Part of the Sol group, near the new marina, with a large swimming pool and air-conditioned rooms – but nothing else available for miles.

Mount Teide

Mount Teide is a dormant volcano, with a huge crater, a plateau of wilderness in the centre of the island. From it, a cable car (not for the nervous) goes right to the very top, pure thin air with appropriately breathtaking views all the way to Africa on a really clear day. Four separate roads wind their way amid marvellous scenery as far as the plateau, so you could go twice and take a different route there and back each time. Definitely one of the best trips anywhere.

Gomera

Linked by ferry from Los Cristianos on Tenerife, an hour and a half by frequent ferry, a fascinating, unspoilt little island with no resorts and no airport. But – you've guessed it – no beaches, either. The Hermigua and Gran Rey valleys offer wonderful scenery, but Gran Rey is at the end of a prodigiously winding road where even the hairpins have hairpins. The chief claim to fame of the capital, San Sebastián, is that Christopher Columbus prepared his ships here, in 1492, on his way to discovering the New World.

EL HIERRO

If the Canaries ever were the tip of the lost continent of Atlantis, then El Hierro might have been where the Atlantan got away from it all – an island so remote that, in the 15th century, cartographers made it (long before Greenwich was ever heard of outside England) 0 degrees longitude, believing that this was where the world began. Although it has an airstrip, and a slightly precarious daily service from Tenerife, El Hierro remains largely unspoilt, with an industry based on agriculture rather than on tourists. Remarkably, however, there is one excellent hotel:

HOTEL Boomerang

No, the owner is not Australian – but he did live down under for a while and made enough money to start up in the hotel business. Located in the tiny town of Valverde, which is built on a hillside so that the local inhabitants could spot potentially unpleasant visitors and make themselves scarce, the Boomerang has 21 rooms, all with bath, and a fine restaurant. Yes, and visitors do come back.

Mount Teide

GRAN CANARIA

The sailors of the world come here to play, while their ships are being refuelled or refurbished in the huge deep water harbour of Las Palmas, from oil tankers to luxury liners, more than 900 a month. But Gran Canaria has much to offer the holidaymaker: beautiful sandy beaches (positively not black), indefatigable night life, and a remarkable transformation in scenery ranging from subtropical valleys to sandy deserts, with a skyline dominated by forbidding mountains. But, like Tenerife, the weather is much more reliable in the south.

Cruz de Tejeda

A stone cross, 4,757 feet above sea level, erected at the central apex of the island's road system, from where the views are memorable. The extraordinary rock formations in a volcanic basin include the Nublo spike, once worshipped as a god. On a clear day you can see the snow-capped peak of Tenerife's Mount Teide, some 60 miles away.

Maspalomas

Three resorts in one, Playa El Oasis, the quietest (though that is only relative) and most attractive; Playa des Inglés, the largest suffering from a severe overdose of concrete; and San Agustin, the smallest but also the scruffiest. In all, ten miles of golden sand on a scale more appropriate to the Sahara Desert, lapped by the sea. If a beach holiday is what you want, rather than local atmosphere, there is none better in the Canary Islands.

HOTEL Royal Maspalomas Oasis

A beautiful location, set among palm trees in a contrived, but tasteful, 'oasis', with a large swimming pool and adjoining tanning yards for those who can't make it to the beach. Tennis, golf, every conceivable amenity. Expensive.

Puerto Rico

A more recent development, constructed in the south-west of the island around a park and a yacht marina, mainly self-catering apartments. The beach is sheltered and safe but becomes crowded in high season.

The house where Columbus stayed

Las Palmas

A day out here need not deprive you of the beach, because Las Palmas has an extremely good one at Puerto de la Luz, free of pollution from the ocean terminal. The Vegueta quarter is full of delightful old Spanish architecture and the Casa de Colón, the residence of the island's first governor, has an interesting museum commemorating the three occasions on which Christopher Columbus was a guest in what is now known, inaccurately, as his house. But for the help he received in the Canary Islands, Columbus might never have reached America, as he needed major repairs to one of his three ships here in 1492. With a sailor's healthy sense of superstition, Columbus stayed here again on his triumphant return from the West Indies (though he still thought they were the East Indies). You can see delightful scale models of his three ships in the museum. That apart, the virtually tax-free shops of Las Palmas remain a considerable attraction, with drink far cheaper than at duty-free airport shops.

LANZAROTE

An island of black lava, the product of volcanic eruptions in the 18th century, the landscape could, almost, belong to another planet. Yet it gives rise to some intriguing excursions both above and below ground, and many of the beaches, despite the volcano, are of golden sand. One which is decidedly grey is the main beach at Playa Blanca, in the most developed tourist area south of the capital, Arrecife. There is, however, another Playa Blanca, mainly apartments, on the southern tip of the island, where, despite major new development, the beaches are more agreeable and much less crowded.

Costa Teguise

Easily the best resort; there is a series of quite tasteful developments, some apartment-based, some hotels, north of Arrecife on the island's eastern coast. Because of the number of swimming pools, the beaches are often surprisingly empty.

HOTEL Las Salinas Sheraton

Completely over the top, the kind of hotel where Tarzan of the Apes would be at home, a tropical garden of plants and creepers which spreads upwards from the uselessly shaped swimming pool to the room balconies (and thereby providing creepy-crawlies with an easy route to the bed . . .).

Montañas de Fuego – the Fire Mountains

Situated in the west of the island, from where the lunar landscape is at its most spectacular, black lava and dark red volcanic hilltops. You can go for a camel ride across the warm cinders, which provide a natural (and cheap) source of heat for cooking in the nearby posh café.

Los Verdes Caves

Los Verdes, in the north of the island, is a cave torn out of the rock by the force of a volcano looking for an exit. It runs for almost four miles through into the sea, and once provided a refuge from the Barbary pirates.

———— ALGARVE ————

The Algarve is the southernmost province of Portugal, full of brilliant colours, Moorish architecture, and beaches which range from placid sandy coves to shores battered by fierce Atlantic rollers. It has the atmosphere and temperatures of the Mediterranean resorts without their garish development, and despite the marked increase in tourism, fishing is still the predominant industry. An ideal choice for a sophisticated beach holiday, although at the height of summer, local facilities are stretched to the limit.

Sagres

The further west you go, the emptier the beaches though the rougher the seas. Sagres was the nerve centre of the Great Discoveries. It was here that Prince Henry, who became known as Henry the Navigator, brought together a formidable group of cartographers and navigators in the 15th century to work out a way of steering a ship (and, incidentally, inventing the first recognisable rudder) out of sight of land.

Previously sailors had used only a compass to determine their course. Now they learned to calculate their latitude from the height of the stars above the horizon. The motive was commercial, the need for a safe sea route to India and the spices of the East beyond the reach of the Barbary pirates; but what Henry set in motion led to the discovery of America and the demonstration that the world was, indeed, round.

HOTEL Pousada do Infante

The equivalents of the Spanish paradors, pousadas are Portuguese state-run hotels which offer exceptional value for money, and are often set, like this one, in wild and beautiful settings. The Pousada do Infante has lovely rooms, fine architecture and an impressive restaurant. Those tempted to make this their base for exploring the Algarve should note, however, that the hotel has only 15 rooms and may limit the length of your stay.

Cape St Vincent

The most southwesterly point on the continent of Europe, offering a huge panoramic view of the Atlantic from the lighthouse at its pinnacle, more than 200 feet above the water. Even in summer, huge waves can often be seen pounding the rocks below.

Praia da Alvor

A quiet little town with an attractive, curved beach, one of the best in the Algarve, set among spectacular rocks. There is a lift to:

HOTEL Alvor Praia

Beautiful surroundings, large swimming pool and a relaxed atmosphere. The best rooms are at the front, with a sea view.

Praia da Rocha

A favourite stopping point for many cruise ships, which anchor offshore. The beach is superb, with remarkable rock formations.

Prince Henry 'The Navigator'

Vale do Lobo

Eight miles west of Faro, a lovely resort in a secluded valley (hence Valley of the Wolf, Vale do Lobo), for once not spoilt by the exceptional luxury hotel built opposite the beach:

HOTEL Dona Filipa

One of the best, if not the best, hotels in Portugal. Superbly appointed rooms, wonderful service, more than adequate swimming pool, excellent food but at the same time an extremely relaxed atmosphere. Expensive, though not for the quality provided.

Vale do Lobo Villas

A luxurious villa complex with communal swimming pool and formidable golf course. Even the supermarket has marble floors. Extremely convenient for Faro airport, less than five miles away. However non-golfing visitors may not feel it is worth the money.

Santa Barbara de Nexe

Five miles from Faro to the north-west and six miles from the sea; notable only for one hotel.

HOTEL La Réserve

Set in large, spacious grounds, with two swimming pools, and air-conditioned rooms arranged as little suites, each with its own tiny kitchen. The restaurant, offering Swiss cooking by the owners, is superb on a good day. Expensive.

Albufeira

Its narrow streets rising steeply from a thriving central square, Albufeira is the place to shop – the most popular resort in the Algarve, but one which has succeeded in keeping its own local identity. From the cliff tops, you can see the rooftops of the town fan out below, and the sea lapping gently on the

Albufeira

sandy beach. To reach it, you have to walk through a rather bizarre tunnel which starts in the centre of town. As the beach is extremely crowded in summer, knowledgeable visitors with transport drive about four miles east to Praia de Falesia, which has a much longer and quieter beach sheltered by lovely sandstone cliffs.

HOTEL Solemar

Built into the cliffs, its rooms provide an exceptional sea view, although entering a hotel on the sixth floor and going down to everything does take a little getting used to. The swimming pool is rather small and you take your chances on the beach or take your car to Praia de Falesia. The hotel is particularly sympathetic towards children and has a very imaginative voucher system that allows you to take half board and eat out at a number of restaurants in the town. Excellent value.

Monchique

From Portimão, a road winds into the hills, in which, unlike Spain where they become increasingly barren, the greenery becomes more and more lush the higher you go. A side road leads to Fóia, a peak that towers over the surrounding countryside and from where, on a clear day, you can see Cape St Vincent 30 miles away. Clear days are, however, comparatively rare, as the secure sunshine of the coast does not reach far inland. Monchique, which you pass through on the way to the peak, is an attractive old market town. The market, open most days in summer, specialises in basket and copperware.

HOTEL Estalagem Abrigo de Montanha

This estalagem, an approved country inn, is a mile outside Monchique on the road towards Fóia, set in a lovely garden overlooking some even lovelier countryside. Family run, home cooking (more or less anything you ask for), with the best rooms, for once, in the annexe at the bottom of the garden. Eccentric and frequently exasperating plumbing, but exceptional value. Coach parties at lunch time.

TUSCANY AND THE ITALIAN RIVIERA

Sunshine, sophisticated beaches and beautiful warm water ensure that the Italian Riviera remains a worthy rival to the French, and is still unimaginably cheaper. On the eastern end of the Gulf of Genoa is a land of hills and cypress trees, a vivid landscape that makes seclusion easy to discover, and within striking distance are the three giants of Renaissance Italy: Pisa, Siena and fabulous Florence.

Diano Marina

Sheltered on the north by the Maritime Alps, this seaside town has a marvellous sandy beach and facilities for every conceivable water sport. The surrounding countryside, olive groves, pine trees and market gardens, adds to its immense charm. One snag: Genoa airport is $2\frac{1}{2}$ hours away.

Grand Hotel Diana Majestic

Any hotel with direct access to its own beach has much to offer, and this hotel is among the best on the beautiful Italian Riviera. The swimming pool is agreeably located so that sunbathers can lie between it and the sea, and on the Majestic beach hotel guests are provided with deckchairs and umbrellas without additional charge. Most of the rooms have a balcony with views of the sea. Excellent restaurant and, in the evening, a piano bar where, for once, the drinks are reasonably priced.

Portofino

The peninsula of Portofino marks the beginning of an exquisitely beautiful coastline, with wonderful views from the promontory over the Gulf of Rapallo and back towards Portofino itself, an enchanting little harbour backed by multi-coloured houses set among the trees. Just into the Gulf and reached by the corniche road – a stunning ride with its marvellous views – is the fashionable yachting centre of Santa Margherita, with an exceptional place to stay:

Grand Hotel Miramare

Set in lush, tropical gardens overlooking the sea, the Miramare, with its vivid white walls and blue shutters, is a luxurious and correspondingly expensive hotel. Its pride and joy is a superb, circular swimming pool with a bar under a splendid canopy where you can drink all day – or until your money runs out.

Sestri Levante

Sestri, a sinuous collection of bright villas and slightly pretentious little shops, offers more than a splendid beach in the middle of a sweeping bay. It is also the ideal centre from which to explore the Cinque Terra (literally five lands – Monterosso, Vernazza, Corniglia, Manarola and Riomaggiore), five coastal villages so isolated that, for many years, they were virtually independent. See if their speciality, a sweet white wine, has the effect its name suggests – sciacchetia, the chattering one.

Grand Hotel Villa Balbi

From the front it looks like a residence of the nobility, a palace of pink and gold, and, indeed, it was in the 18th century, until the family fell on hard times. If you are lucky you can sleep in their very bedrooms, with vast, marble bathrooms, though most of the accommodation is in the larger, modern extension. Not many of the rooms have much of a view of the sea, which is a little surprising, as the hotel stands right on the sea front, with its own section of private beach across the road. There is a lovely swimming pool, with a shallow section for children, in the leafy grounds. The restaurant is excellent, providing a wide variety of cuisine.

Marina di Pietrasanta

Very much a resort patronised by the Italian middle class, so an air of quiet self-assurance pervades this charming little seaside town. The beach of fine sand stretches for miles. Almost everyone seems to be engaged in the seasonal occupation of letting or servicing villas and apartments, most of which are

Portofino

within easy walking distance of the sea; few, though, have swimming pools or large gardens. For a hotel, try the adjacent resort Forte dei Marmi which has an attractive pedestrian-free promenade, and even a pier:

HOTEL Tirreno

Located close to an excellent beach, this hotel has an outstanding garden in which to sunbathe, and some (but by no means all) of the rooms enjoy a balcony with a sea view. Extremely friendly establishment, run by a family for whom nothing is too much trouble. Eat out.

Panzano

A small village set on a hillside in Tuscany, equidistant from Florence or Siena, each 30 minutes drive. The vineyards which produce the grape of Chianti Classico are prolific here, but the village would be of little consequence were it not for its hotel:

Villa Le Barone

Owned by the Duchess Visconti and once the property of the famous Tuscan family, Della Robbia, it is still a private home for much of the year. The outside appearance is striking, vivid white walls with ascending greenery, and the interior superbly furnished. However, the grounds, despite the existence of a swimming pool, are surprisingly claustrophobic. The restaurant is in the old wine cellar, too far from the kitchens, and were it practical, the advice would be to eat elsewhere. The other pitfall is its distance from the nearest airport, Pisa, a good three hours' drive away.

San Gimignano

Medieval skyscrapers, 13 in number, the survivors of more than 60, dominate this extraordinary relic of the 14th century, when the towers were built as a means of defence during family feuds and as a measure of prestige. The complete city wall has survived, encircling the narrow streets of old houses and splendid palaces. Despite the large number of visitors, the atmosphere is truly remarkable, worth a considerable journey to see. San Gimignano is 27 miles south-west of Florence, 19 north-east of Siena, but there is a hotel:

HOTEL Bel Soggiorno

A vast window dominates one wall of the restaurant, offering unparalleled views of the Tuscan countryside and almost enough to make you forget the food, except that it is extremely imaginative. The rooms all have baths, but some are rather small and consequently stifling in summer. Young children seem welcome in the restaurant, but not to stay the night: perhaps the owner is a light sleeper. One thing is certain, he hates credit cards, and will only accept one from the destitute.

Florence

A city so totally immersed in art it saturates the senses. The Uffizi Museum has strong claims to be the best in the world. It contains the Botticelli Room, with three remarkable works: the 'Birth of Venus', 'Spring' and 'Madonnas'; and a matchless piece of Greek sculpture, the Medici Venus. The Piazza della Signoria is an open-air museum, because there are far too many statues to be housed inside. The cathedral dome, a masterpiece by Brunelleschi, took 14 years of his life; it is almost as high as St Paul's. So how was this collective genius gathered and nurtured here in this city of Leonardo de Vinci and Michaelangelo? Through commerce. Guilds such as the clothmakers, who paid for the cathedral, and the jewellers, whose descendents still sell their intricately worked gold and jewels on the exquisite Ponte Vecchio spanning the River Arno, were enlightened patrons of the arts. But the key to the power of medieval Florence was lending money: bank drafts were invented here. One of the first clients was King John, to pay for a mercenary army to secure his throne when Richard the Lionheart died.

Siena (see page 24)

Pisa

Once a powerful city state, the grandeur of Pisa can best be seen by entering the cathedral square from the west – a striking combination of the cathedral, the beautiful baptistry and the famous Leaning Tower. Why does it lean? The architect, Bonnano Pisano, tried to make out that he did it on purpose. If he did, then he lived dangerously for, ever since, the best minds in Italy have devoted considerable energy to making certain that it stays up . . . not altogether successfully, as it leans a little more each year. The upper part, built by Pisano's successors, is vertical, which is just as well because otherwise it would have fallen over long ago. The tilt is probably due to a defect in the foundations or to the settling of the subsoil. Whatever the cause, the effect is quite uncanny when you reach the second spiral of its staircase, giving a sensation that you are about to fall. Only Galileo, who was born in Pisa, found any real use for it: by leaning out of the Leaning Tower, he could drop objects to the ground to show how the speed of their fall depended directly on their weight – the laws of gravitation demonstrated to the world.

—THE GREEK ISLANDS—

Greece is the land of a thousand islands, where the clock runs slowly and the dreamy days seem to stretch into infinity. Although mass tourism has edged its way into the larger resorts, the logic and logistics of the Greek way of life still confound the package tour planners. Communications, at any rate by sea, are a matter of supreme improvisation, with arrival and departure times bearing no resemblance whatsoever to the timetable which seems largely the figment of someone's fertile imagination. The food, at best uninspired, is transformed simply by the supreme pleasure of eating it outside in evocative little ports and watching the sun go down over the bright blue sea. New airports have opened up the way to many islands which would other-

Greek Islands

Corfu • Limnos • Athens • Delos • Mykonos • Antiparos • Paros • Patmos • Kalymnos • Kos • Santorini • Rhodes • Karpathos • Crete

0   50   100   150   200
Kilometres

wise have been out of reach to all but those with opportunities to take really long holidays. If you do travel through Athens, visit it first, and unwind elsewhere.

Rhodes

The towering fortress of the Knights of St John is a reminder of how Rhodes was once the last Christian outpost in the eastern Mediterranean, defended by the fanatical Knights of St John until the Turks finally took it in 1522. Today's invaders are all tourists, too many for comfort especially in July and August. If you can come out of peak season the island is transformed, and you can enjoy its agreeable bays and beaches. The best is probably at Lindos, a delightful village set on the hillside in evocative scenery, although it is now a mecca for tourists, with rows of cafés offering all-day bacon and eggs. The village has many apartments and villas to rent, but if you must have a hotel, there are two round the headland in the adjoining bay.

Kalymnos

Lush green valleys and severe mountain escarpments are the highlights of Kalymnos, an island accessible only by ferry from Rhodes or Kos, where most tourists are Greek. Sponge fishing is the principal activity. Accommodation is largely basic, even in the hotels on the fine bay around Massouri and Myrties. Transport is by shared taxi, mainly old Mercedes, generally an accident that has already found somewhere to happen. Animal lovers may find the number of half-starved stray cats rather disturbing.

Patmos

An exceptionally beautiful island, perhaps the most beautiful in the Aegean, Patmos has deep sheltered bays and lush, inland greenery. In the south, the village of Chora is a truly exceptional picture: white walls, cobbles, lovely houses, all dominated by an ancient fortified monastery. The best beach is at Grikou, unless you hire a boat and go to the more inaccessible parts of the island.

Knossos, Crete

Crete

A large island which possesses places of such interest that it simply cannot be missed. When our ancestors were still living in caves, the Cretans had established a remarkable civilisation. Some of the archaeological sites on the island go back about 4,000 years, and there are two of epic significance, the Minoan Palaces at Phaestos and Knossos. In this land of rugged mountains reflecting the blazing sun, the existence of the Gods somehow no longer seems implausible. As King Minos undoubtedly lived, and the Minoans did indeed worship the sacred bull, is the legend of Theseus and the Minotaur so unlikely? At Knossos, reconstructed to provide a plausible glimpse of what Minoan civilisation may have looked like at its peak, they had flushing toilets and constant hot water, which alas cannot be said of every hotel or guest house on the island thousands of years later.

If you are to make the most of Crete, hiring a car is essential. The international firms are easily undercut by the islanders, but their cars need to be gone over with the proverbial toothcomb to make sure that they are in good working order. All of them are treated appallingly, because the state of the roads, especially inland, would be enough to make a discriminating donkey stop in his tracks.

Elounda

The feeling of 'déjà vu' on arrival is probably explained by the fact that the resort once provided the charming backcloth for a television drama, "Who Pays The Ferryman?" Perhaps as a consequence, Elounda has lost its out-of-the-way charm and become a bustling, fashionable holiday centre with smart discothèques and restaurants. Picturesque . . . at a price.

HOTEL Elounda Beach

East of the town, too far to walk, not that many guests here would be unable to afford a taxi. Luxurious air-conditioned rooms and bungalow apartments set in substantial grounds. A large swimming pool compensates for the rather indifferent beach. Unusually for a luxury hotel, children are unreservedly made welcome. Huge programme of activities day and night, including sailing and surfing classes.

Karpathos

Many tourists' only recollection of Karpathos may be that it provided an interlude of blissful escape on a rough crossing between Crete and Rhodes, for the Aegean is by no means always just a rippled sea.

Situated almost exactly halfway between Crete and Rhodes, Karpathos has somehow seemed to take pleasure in being inaccessible. For a long time it had no airport and relied on a ferry which was always full of lorries and never had room for tourist cars. Anyone hiring a car in Crete or Rhodes with the intention of taking it to Karpathos (local hire is difficult in season) is well advised to equip himself with at least one extra tyre. Karpathos is split in two by a spectacular mountain range, something akin to the spine of a dinosaur, and the road across, endlessly winding and a series of potholes, was definitely not built by the Romans. An additional hazard is the number of Greek-Americans with battered Chevrolets, who drive as though they are on the freeway.

It is, though, essential to get to the north, if only to visit the village of Olympos lying just beneath the barren peaks, where the

Bali

Fishing is still the principal industry in this remote, unspoilt village between Heraklion and Rethymon. Rugged countryside, tiny, agreeable beach . . . but the name itself is a potentially wonderful piece of one-upmanship when the neighbours ask where you went on holiday.

HOTEL Bali Beach

Apartment complex set in the hillside overlooking the sea at the back. Secluded, relaxing, but very little to do in the evenings; car essential.

inhabitants still wear traditional costume and speak in a dialect that would be just as incomprehensible to an Athenian as it is to you. It is an island of breathtaking scenery and superb beaches, the finest being near Lefkos and best reached by fisherman's caique; don't pay for the return trip in advance. The hotels offer bed and breakfast; but islanders' rooms are often more agreeable and much better value.

Kos

A lively, interesting island with an international airport, Kos is now unashamedly commercial, and has a vibrant night life. Its ancient remains include a mosque, a reminder of centuries of Turkish rule. The Turks dislodged the Knights of St John: the massive walls of their fortress survive in Kos Town. So does a vast plane tree, said to have belonged to Hippocrates, not the mathematician who invented geometry, but the founder of scientific medicine, under whom Kos became a medical centre and received patients from all over Ancient Greece. Today, it is the beaches which excel, especially at Kardemena, the remote Kamari and in the south, Aghios Stefanos and simply Paradise. Should you come from Athens and not wish to fly, the ferry includes an overnight journey and takes, in all, 14 hours.

Limnos

On-duty fishermen and off-duty soldiers make up most of the population of Limnos, whose main port, Myrina, with its ruined fortress, is the only lively spot. However, the beaches are excellent in the south, and just along the bay is an outstanding hotel:

HOTEL Akti Myrina

Secluded bungalows dotted around a hillside, each with its own private patio garden, and all within a few minutes' walk of the beach and the central complex of swimming pool and restaurants, make up this luxurious hotel. It has a superb setting, and equally superb food. Expensive. Limnos can be reached by air from Athens or, on a rather long haul, by ferry.

Mykonos

Perhaps the most picturesque, and certainly the most fashionable, of all the Greek islands, despite its reputation for being populated by gays. The town has a wonderful stretch of timber houses, which overhang the water, called Little Venice; and a harbour with a pulsating night-life, discos and live groups tucked away in cafés in the maze of alleyed streets. The food is superior to that found in the other islands.

Delos

An uninhabited island, reached from Mykonos, Delos is noted for its lions – fortunately of the stone variety, which stand guard over the great ruined palace that was once a centre of Greek civilisation. In Greek mythology, Leto, seduced by Zeus, was forced to wander from place to place by the jealous Hera until she found respite in Delos and gave birth to Zeus's son, Apollo, beside a palm tree.

Paros

Popular, perhaps too popular in the summer, because Paros lies on an easily accessible ferry route from Piraeus, the port of Athens. Parikia, the main port, can be extremely noisy and crowded. Elsewhere, however, there are quiet, sandy beaches, especially in the south east. For those not unduly concerned with the quality of their accommodation, Piso Livadi is the ideal place to stay. However the best hotel is:

HOTEL Xenia

The famous white marble of Paros, which was used to build the temples on Delos, is also here in abundance – floors, staircases, ceilings. The hotel stands on a hill above Parikia village, overlooking the beach, and is just far enough away to see the bright lights of the evening without being kept awake by the music, which goes on late into the night. The rooms are extremely comfortable, the best having a balcony and a sea view; the hotel takes most credit cards.

Mykonos

Lions of Delos

Antiparos

A creaking caique takes visitors from bustling Paros to the idyllic little island of Antiparos with its sheltered lagoon. You can take a memorable trip up into the hills, by donkey, and down into a huge cavern of stalagmites and stalactites where the temperature is cool and constant no matter how sweltering the day.

Santorini

The Minoan civilisation came to an end when Santorini, sometimes called Thira, was torn apart 3,500 years ago by volcanic eruption. Popular mythology would have us believe that the same cataclysm engulfed Atlantis, the lost island of the gods, which still survives somewhere, beneath the waters of the Aegean. After Knossos, nothing can be dismissed lightly. Whatever Thira was, visiting ships sail close by the volcanic crater, a sheer cliff with superb views from the top.

The town of Thira is brash and commercialised, a reflection of the number of cruise ships which call. Most visitors take the predictable excursion by donkey to the volcano; fewer see the fascinating excavations of the Minoan city at Akrotiri.

The most interesting place to stay is at Ia, a village to the north, perched high above the sea with many of its houses in ruins, the eerie result of a much more recent convulsion, this time an earthquake on land. Stay there at:

HOTEL Atlantis Villas

A chance to become a troglodite, although the caves have kitchens and bathrooms, in traditional island dwellings restored by the owner. Bed and breakfast only, but a splendid bar and a sea-water swimming pool with a sun terrace which is of particular advantage, as the island has only black, volcanic beaches – one of the few shortcomings of Santorini. Hotel closed November to February.

Corfu

Ulysses may have come here; the Venetians, the French and the British certainly did, giving Corfu its unique character – the Greek island closest to Western Europe.

There is not a shred of archaeological evidence to support it, but Ulysses is supposed to have been shipwrecked on Corfu on his way home from the Trojan War; the story goes that he was washed ashore naked and unconscious, to be found by Princess Nausicaa, who liked what she saw sufficiently to take him back to her father King Alcinous. The King had no desire to have Ulysses as a son-in-law, and quickly provided a boat to send him on his way.

The Palace of King Alcinous is popularly supposed to have been at Paleokastrítsa, the jewel in Corfu's crown, a breathtaking panorama of wooded promontories and hidden coves lapped by a deep blue sea, with a 16th-century monastery leaning over the cliff edge as though in sheer amazement at the beauty of its surroundings.

Also on Corfu's west coast, but further south, is another monastery, Mirtiótissa, on a superb beach, jagged cliffs and huge boulders running into the sand like the debris left after a quarrel among the gods, but so isolated it takes a determined traveller to find it. Like many of Corfu's most enticing stretches of sand, it is most easily reached by boat – indeed there are many beaches quite inaccessible by any other form of transport.

Fortunately, on Corfu there are boats aplenty for hire, much better value than the retinue of scooters and motor-assisted bicycles lent, without crash helmets, all too often to inexperienced riders, some of whom may be unfortunate enough to sample Corfu's free health care. Hire cars are in short supply and correspondingly expensive.

The island's biggest problem is the sheer number of tourists in high season, when finding a hotel room or a villa to rent can be extremely difficult at short notice. Against that, the people are relaxed and friendly, and rather better than most foreigners at understanding the British mentality – a legacy, perhaps, of the 19th century, when having chucked out the Napoleonic French, the British set up shop here themselves for exactly 50 years. They left behind a cricket pitch of sparse grass with a wicket closer to concrete than clay. Prudent holidaymakers who fancy a game first make sure that there are no genuine fast bowlers in the party.

HOTEL Margarona Palace

On the main road into Dassia on the east coast, a large, modern, air-conditioned hotel which would be taken for granted in many resort areas but is of startling quality for Corfu. Large swimming pool, with separate section and many other facilities for children. Agreeable gardens, spacious public rooms, attractive restaurant. Live music most nights, and always a disco.

YUGOSLAVIA'S —DALMATION COAST—

Four out of every five visitors to Yugoslavia stay on the Adriatic coast, influenced by its exceptional weather: it is warmer and, almost invariably, sunnier, than many of the traditional destinations in the Mediterranean. The Dalmation coast is, also, a region of outstanding scenic beauty; add to this the walls of Dubrovnik and the Diocletian temple at Split, and you have a hugely interesting and attractive holiday.

Gulf of Kotor

Close by the international airport which serves Dubrovnik, lies a series of intricate bays which, but for the temperate climate, could be part of the Norwegian fiords. At the foot of the almost sheer cliffs of Mount Lovćen (nearly 6,000 ft) is Kotor, whose fortifications were woven, amazingly, into the rockface. They survived several sieges, only to be threatened by a recent earthquake, which damaged Kotor's marvellous Gothic cathedral. Opposite Perast, where the Venetians recruited the most skilful of their sailors, is the small island of Gospa od Skrpjela, with a

Harbour at Dubrovnik

tiny baroque church which was constructed in the 15th century, stone by stone on an underwater reef – a remarkable project. After the decline of the Venetian Republic, Perast became a naval power in her own right in the 17th century. The machinations of Balkan politics took some of their ships as far as the Baltic to help Czar Peter the Great against Sweden. On the northern shore, the sophisticated resort of Hercegovni has another collection of ruined forts, put up by various masters, but is most famous for its displays of flowers in spring and early summer. Just south of the Gulf, the empty, ruined town of Budva sits on the water's edge, its red roofs and white watchtower visible for miles, surrounded by massive fortifications built by the Venetians in the 15th century to protect their trade routes. Most of the modern hotels are situated in Bečići, two miles to the south, with colourful gardens close by a coarse, sandy beach, but it is also possible to sleep in a medieval atmosphere:

HOTELS

Sveti Stefan

A fortified village connected to the shore by a narrow causeway. When it was effectively abandoned as a base by the local fishing community, because they found the water too shallow for their boats, the Yugoslav government took it over as a unique tourist complex. You can stay in the 16th-century houses, beautifully preserved and providing first-class accommodation. Sveti Stefan has several shops, a fine restaurant and even a night-club.

Avala

The original hotel, built at Budva in 1935, was a regular haunt of exiled rulers and, reputedly, spies. Its modern replacement lacks the atmosphere of its predecessor but has the same advantageous location, managing to be both next to the beach and in the town centre. There are two swimming pools, one indoor, and the alternative of self-catering apartments on the adjoining hillside, linked with the Avala.

Dubrovnik

A medieval city state, preserved by playing off the great powers one with another and, for good measure, building a city wall so formidable that any army would be hard put to breach it. The 15th-century fortifications are almost perfectly preserved, offering a truly extraordinary glimpse of spires, towers and secluded courtyards.

If the bastions and turrets deterred the enemy without, the citizens of Dubrovnik always feared the enemy within. The city was run by three councils, presided over by a Rector, who held office for only one month at a time. He was given a splendid Palace in which to live, but was not allowed outside its walls during his short-lived time in power. The Sponza Palace houses the documents of diplomacy up to the 19th century, including the undertaking given by Napoleon to preserve Dubrovnik's independence. The ink was scarcely dry on the parchment when he sent his army to take the city.

HOTEL Villa Dubrovnik

Built, with extraordinary ingenuity, into the cliff on the south side of Dubrovnik, the Villa has superb views of the old city and many rooms with sea views from lovely little balconies. Bathing is possible from a secluded set of rocks, and the hotel runs a taxi-boat service into town. The restaurant, which has equally superb views over the sea and the town, offers a high standard of cuisine.

Split

The city owes its origins to the Roman emperor Diocletian, who built a palace here at the end of the 3rd century AD; he abdicated and came to live in it. Of all the explanations for his choice, the most attractive, and in some ways the most plausible in view of his advancing senility, was that the soil was ideal for growing cabbages – and growing cabbages, as Lewis Carroll might have expected, was Diocletian's hobby. His palace has had bits built on and bits borrowed over the centuries; all attempts have been given up to preserve it from the ravages of the tourist. You can have a drink at cafés set up right inside it, anathema for the archaeological purist, no doubt, but enormously appealing to the casual visitor. He or she will need to conserve their energy if they decide on an excursion to Klis, five miles to the east, a lofty fortress guarding the pass between the Kozjak and Mosor mountains; three sets of walls circle the heights and, though the climb is exhausting, the view is worth it.

HOTEL Lav

Unfortunately named for British visitors, but the Lav is, nevertheless, a first-class hotel located five miles outside the city beside the sea. It has its own harbour, a restaurant on the beach and an indoor swimming pool (closed in July and August, because no one bothers to use it in fine weather). If you find the Lav's size a little daunting, there are self-catering apartments in the grounds, which allow you to use all the hotel facilities.

Islands

The longest island in the Adriatic, Hvar, is also one of the most beautiful. Forty-three miles in length, it has vineyards and palm trees, and a climate which matches that of Madeira. Hvar Town has medieval mansions and winding streets and at one time gave winter shelter in its deep water harbour to the Venetian fleet. Korčula Island, much closer to the mainland, consists mainly of a delightful old fortified city. Its outstanding building is St Mark's Cathedral, though one tall house with a watchtower is claimed, with little concrete evidence, to be the birthplace of Marco Polo. Korčula is also noted for the continued survival of wild jackal, so for tourists to stray outside the elaborately carved city gates may be unwise after dark.

HOTEL Palace, Hvar

Once a Venetian palace, it has been turned into an extremely comfortable hotel with an indoor swimming pool and a splendid terrace. The best rooms have a view over the harbour of Hvar, but it is not particularly close to any pleasant beaches.

CHAPTER 4

BEST BEACHES

On package tours, the quality of the beach is of overwhelming importance for the great majority of holidaymakers. Information about good beaches is rather more difficult to discover, in advance, than information about hotels. Not all the beaches mentioned have appeared in the chapter on the most popular resort areas, as the nearby hotels and excursions may be of limited appeal.

——— SPAIN ———

Costa Brava

Rosas
Gentle sloping, sandy, safe bathing

Estartit
Firm sand, ideal for sand castles

Tossa de Mar
Fine sand, good emergency facilities, but a strong current – children and poor swimmers should be wary

San Pol
A charge is made to go on part of it, very unusual in Spain, but the facilities are excellent

Costa Dorada

Castelldefels
Superb stretch of sand, but too popular with the Spanish at weekends; good safety precautions

San Carlos de la Rápida
The Playa del Juanito, a long, flat sandy beach, has outstanding safety precautions

Costa Blanca

Benidorm
Long stretches of clean, white sand with lifeguards in attendance

Torrevieja
White sand, safe bathing; outstanding cleanliness of beach and facilities

Costa del Sol

Nerja
Several small but excellent beaches, rarely crowded

Malaga
El Palo beach, exceptional sands, energetic lifeguards

Majorca

Alcùdia
Extremely long, sandy, clean beach in picturesque setting

Cala Millor
Fine stretch of sand, gentle slope; backed by long promenade; good first-aid facilities

Minorca

Santandria
Gently sloping sandy beach at end of long rocky inlet

Cala de Santa Galdana
Safe sandy beach with good standard of cleanliness in main swimming area

Cala Pregonda
Isolated sandy bay tucked into the hills on the northern coast

Cala de Santa Galdana, Minorca

Ibiza

San Vicente
Clean sand, very safe for swimming

Formentera
Superb sandy beaches

Tenerife

Puerto de la Cruz
Las Teresitas beach, fine sand (imported from Morocco!) but crowded in season

Gran Canaria

Maspalomas
Miles of golden sand, clean and well equipped with sports and other facilities

Las Palmas
Puerto de la Luz beach is excellent, free of pollution

Puerto Rico
Magnificent beach, sheltered and safe, with an artificial breakwater

Lanzarote

Playa Blanca
Beware confusion with main beach resort near Arrecife; this Playa Blanca is in the south, where beaches have pleasant white sand

PORTUGAL

Algarve

Praia do Martinhal
Quiet stretch of sand east of Sagres, but no facilities

Praia da Rocha
Superb long beach, remarkable rock formations, but crowded in season

Attractive curved beach sheltered by cliffs
at the superior eastern end

Praia de Falesia
Long, quiet beach sheltered by sandstone
cliffs

Praia do Lobo
Despite red cliffs behind, quite exposed;
excellent facilities but crowded in summer

ITALY

Italian Riviera and Tuscany

Diano Marina
Fine sandy beach

Sestri Levante
Splendid beach in sweeping bay

Marina di Pietrasanta
Fine beach stretching for miles

Adriatic

Rimini
Long, sandy beach, very safe swimming;
excellent facilities

Venice Lido
An island opposite Venice with fine, if
over-organised, beaches opposite the major
hotels; safe bathing. Not to be confused with
Lido di Jesolo, some 25 miles south of
Venice.

YUGOSLAVIA

Dalmatian coast

Srebreno
South of Dubrovnik; fine sand with trees
running down to the beach, narrow, but
lovely

Budva
Long, gently sloping sandy beach bordered
by rocks

Bečići
Coarse sand but a fine beach with
mountain scenery behind; safe swimming,
though crowded in season

Miločer
Attractive sandy bay with red-roofed
houses clustered round; ideal for swimming

GREEK ISLANDS

Karpathos

Ammopi and Arkesia have fine sandy
beaches; less accessible beach near Lefkos,
best reached by boat

Rhodes

Lindos has one of the best beaches on the
island, but it is very crowded in high
season

Patmos
Best beach at Grikou, unless you hire a boat

Limnos
Akti Myrina has an outstanding private
beach; there are fine alternatives on the
south-west coast

Paros
Quiet, sandy beaches in south-west

Antiparos
Beautiful sheltered lagoon; regular caique
from Paros

Kos
Outstanding beaches, just north of the town
of Kos, at Kardemena and, in the south,
Aghios Stefanos and Paradise Beach, a
description for once almost justified

Crete
On the north-eastern tip of the island, Vái
has superb sand and a fringe of palm trees

Praia da Rocha, Algarve

CHAPTER 5

CRUISES

General Galtieri should really be made an honorary Board member of Cunard and P & O, as, albeit unintentionally, he did more than anyone to revive the romantic notion of cruising to and from Southampton or some other British port. The role played by *Canberra* and the *QEII* in the Falklands was of enormous significance, and the publicity both ships received helped to slow, if not completely reverse, the trend towards joining cruises by air in distant parts.

The perfectionist will tell you that the only true cruise is one where luggage, rather than money, is no problem. If you follow their example, when the boat train deposits you at Southampton you will need a retinue of porters to transport your belongings to your cabin. No matter how large and sumptuous it may be, you then find that you have more luggage than can possibly be stowed away, and the overflow has to go into the hold until you run out of evening gowns or tuxedos.

Apart from leaving room for what you buy abroad, luggage does of course depend on the extent to which you intend to dress up while on board ship. For men, the problem may be one of shaking the mothballs out of an ancient dinner jacket, and then giving it more use in a fortnight than it has had in several years. For women, a decision on whether they can be seen in the same outfit twice. Few, if any, ships insist on more than collar and tie for dinner, but you may feel out of place if everyone else is in evening dress.

If this obsession with dressing up seems out of date, the educated cruise passenger appreciates that it goes hand in hand with choosing your ship. The dining room is the nerve centre of any cruise, where your stomach, seas permitting, will compel you to spend much time consuming and, probably, almost as much time discussing, the meals you have taken/missed/enjoyed/hated during the voyage. If you dislike your cabin intensely, it may well be possible to change it; if the food is tasteless and the restaurant service indifferent, you are stuck with it.

All the cruise lines promise quantity. On most ships it is quite possible to have Continental breakfast in your cabin, full breakfast in the dining room, elevenses on deck, lunch inside or outside or both, afternoon tea, dinner and, as you will be quite ravenous by then, midnight supper.

Quality is more difficult to assess. Brochure food always looks superb; at least one cruise line plans a half-hour period into its schedule for passengers to take pictures of the deck buffet, so large and spectacular does it look. However, after a fortnight in some ships, passengers find the style of cooking repetitious and predictable. One answer may lie in whether the restaurant or restaurants can take all the passengers at one sitting, as they can, for example, in Cunard's *Vistafjord* or in the fleet of the Royal Viking Line. On these ships, the kitchen and restaurant staff are under less pressure, so the food is served in a more relaxed manner.

Most ships are now one class throughout, but still practise subtle and not so subtle distinctions by allocating restaurants according to the quality of your accommodation. On the *QEII*, for example, there is a large restaurant, with two sittings when the ship is full, called the Tables of the World, a smaller and more select restaurant called the Columbia with one sitting and, finally, if you have paid enough, you will eat in the superb Princess Grill and Queen's Grill. In the *Canberra*, though there is not a great deal of distinction between the menus, passengers in the superior, low-numbered cabins are seated in the Pacific Restaurant and the remainder in the Atlantic Restaurant.

Rather more vital, unless you are seated in a really select restaurant, may be your choice of the sitting and of your table. Experienced cruisers tend to choose second sitting because first is far too early and has a set time limit – borne out by the fact that whilst the ship's officers will, happily, preside over large tables for the second sitting, their appearance at the first sitting will be only a token gesture. More agonising is the choice of tables. The only satisfactory table is one for the size of your party, disregarding friends who may be on the same cruise. Your enthusiasm for sitting with them may wane before long – there is a limit to everyone's conversational repertoire. Whether you can achieve the table of your choice is, of course, another matter. It may depend on your clout, your status in the accommodation stakes, and, perhaps, your potential ability to make a nuisance of yourself. What you can be sure is that those passengers who make no effort to stipulate a size and location of table will be stuck on the

biggest, with the most geriatric passengers, and the closest to the kitchen.

Of course if your cabin is luxurious enough, such as the penthouse suites on the *QEII* or one of the Royal Viking ships, you can have your meals in complete privacy in your own cabin, served by your own personal butler.

Cruise lines offer a significant advantage over hotels: they provide detailed plans of their accommodation, so that you can see whether the cabin they propose to give you is close to the cinema, the disco, the engines, or any other part of the ship likely to increase the noise or the temperature. Some ships suffer from serious vibration problems, so, if you can afford it, a cabin on the higher decks well away from the propellors will be much more comfortable.

One common dilemma faced by potential passengers is whether to book a cheap cabin on a more expensive ship, or to opt for a more costly cabin on a cheaper cruise. Experience shows that, for most passengers, the better the cabin the better the holiday. People tend to underestimate both the time that they spend in their cabin, and, for example, the disadvantages of an inside cabin without a porthole which, despite air conditioning, tends to be claustrophobic and aggravate seasickness. The 'court' cabins, invented by P&O and available, for example, on the *Canberra*, avoid this problem. Each 'court' cabin looks out into a small courtyard with a large window in the ship's side, so that it benefits from a glimpse of the sky and some natural light. Only in the more modern and most luxurious ships, such as those of the Royal Viking fleet, are baths rather than showers standard fittings throughout.

If you are in really luxurious accommodation, the temptation may be to remain in splendid isolation, but for most cruisers the amenities of the ship are of considerable importance. Unless the swimming pools are large and numerous, expect them to be crowded when the ship is at sea; if the lounges are not exceptionally big, the available seating for evening entertainment is likely to be taken up entirely by the first sitting

Island Room, Canberra

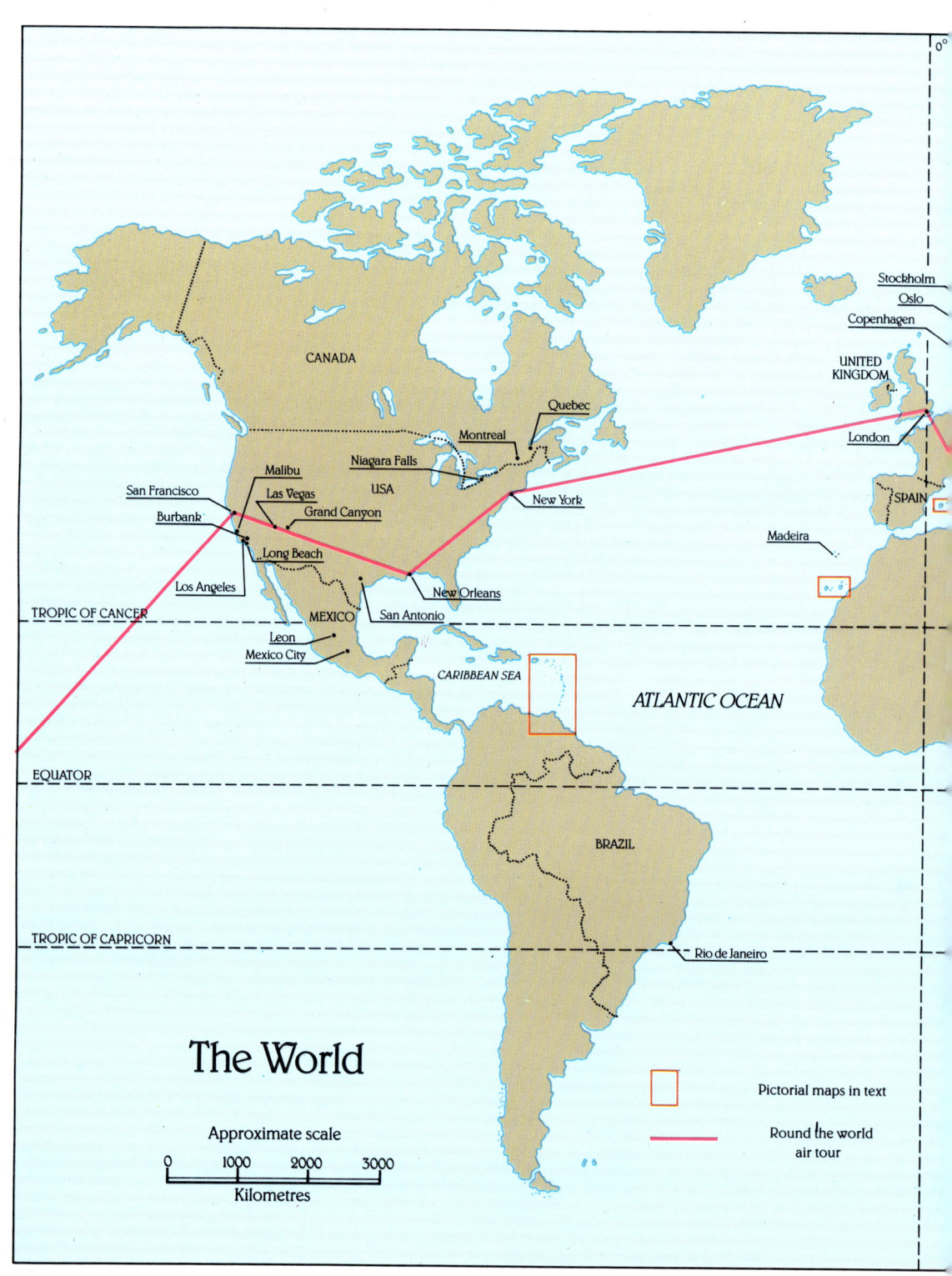

Stockholm
Oslo
Copenhagen

UNITED
KINGDOM

London

CANADA

Quebec

Montreal

Niagara Falls

USA

New York

SPAIN

San Francisco

Malibu

Las Vegas

Burbank

Grand Canyon

Madeira

Long Beach

Los Angeles

New Orleans

TROPIC OF CANCER

MEXICO

San Antonio

Leon

Mexico City

CARIBBEAN SEA

ATLANTIC OCEAN

EQUATOR

BRAZIL

TROPIC OF CAPRICORN

Rio de Janeiro

The World

Approximate scale

0   1000   2000   3000

Kilometres

Pictorial maps in text

Round the world
air tour

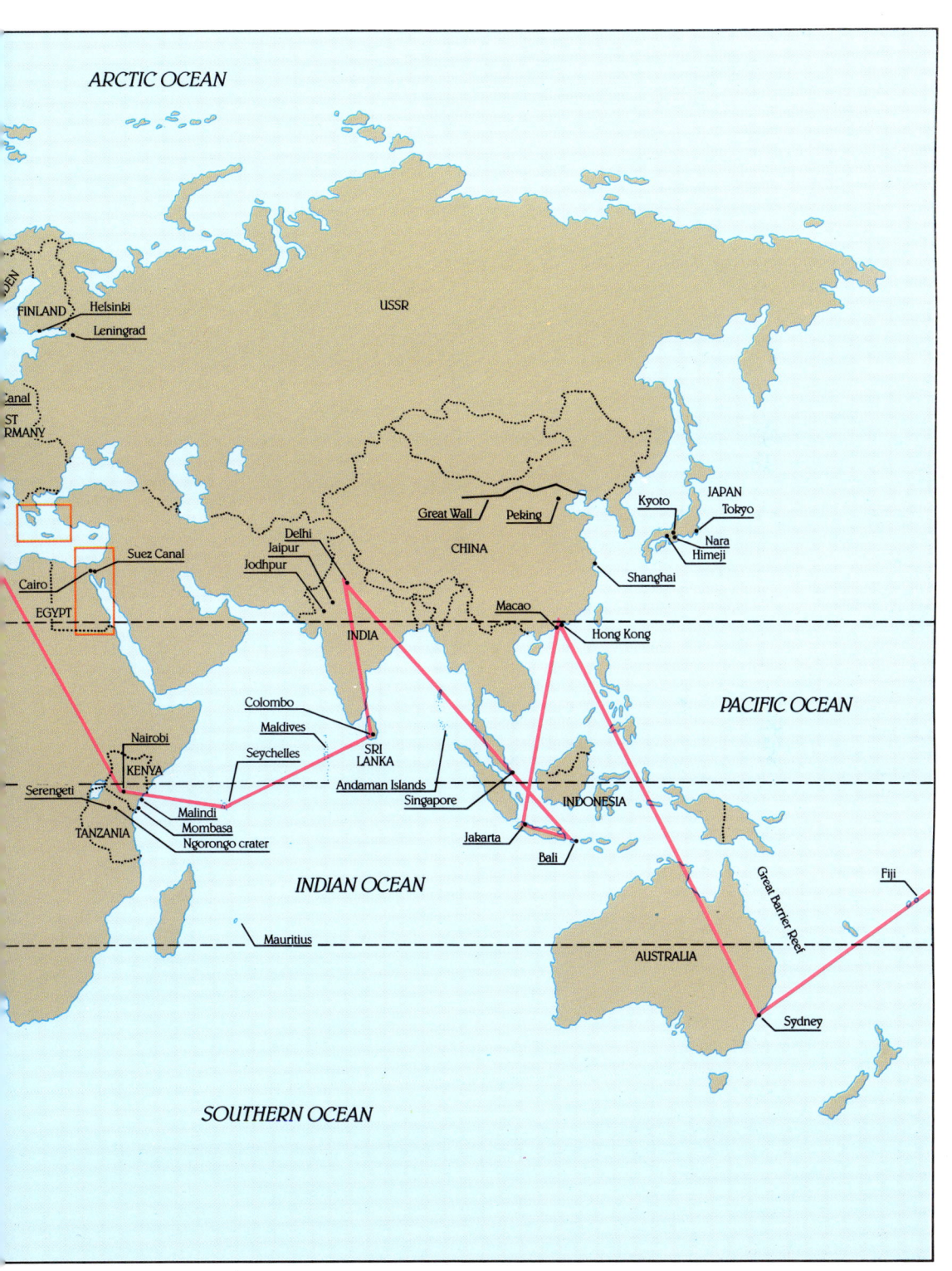

ARCTIC OCEAN

FINLAND Helsinki
Leningrad

USSR

Canal
ST
RMANY

JAPAN
Tokyo
Kyoto

Great Wall   Peking   CHINA

Nara
Himeji

Shanghai

Delhi
Jaipur
Jodhpur

Suez Canal

Cairo
EGYPT

Macao

INDIA

Hong Kong

PACIFIC OCEAN

Colombo
Maldives
Seychelles

Nairobi
KENYA

SRI
LANKA

Serengeti

Malindi
Mombasa
Ngorongo crater

TANZANIA

Andaman Islands
Singapore

INDONESIA

Jakarta

Bali

INDIAN OCEAN

Great Barrier Reef

Fiji

Mauritius

AUSTRALIA

Sydney

SOUTHERN OCEAN

passengers, straight after dinner.

Even passengers able to afford a penthouse suite may welcome the ambience of a big ship, the range of facilities and number of co-passengers, which is why *Sea Goddess I* and *Sea Goddess II*, two of the most expensive cruise liners, may not suit everyone. The accommodation is truly exclusive; every passenger has a suite with a sea view, a sitting room and a full-sized bath. There are video facilities in each cabin together with a complimentary bar – complimentary, that is, if you disregard the price of the cruise.

Sea Goddess Cruises operate in the Caribbean and the Mediterranean, but you have to make your own way (and at your own expense) to and from one of their ships, neither of which is really large enough to sail the Atlantic in comfort. Cruises out of British ports, unless you have a great deal of time to spare, are mainly limited to Scandinavia, the Mediterranean and the Atlantic Islands, and unless you go north to the fjords or the Baltic, your ship will have to pass twice through the Bay of Biscay. Although less than a day's sail from Southampton, it can be rough in summer, and provide seas of terrifying proportions during the winter. Going further afield, for example to the West Indies, takes the best part of a month and involves two very long passages without ports of call, tolerable, in good weather, on the outward leg with the anticipation of sights to come, but a huge anti-climax on the way back. The Caribbean is much better suited to a fly-cruise, for all its shortcomings on the amount of luggage you can take.

Potentially the most successful cruises are those where the ports of call could not be visited in the same time scale by any other means of transport without extreme difficulty – such as the islands of the West Indies, the cities of the Baltic, and the passage through the Suez Canal into the Red Sea. Of course, if you are one of that rare breed of passenger that delights in cruising uninterrupted by ports of call, and who stoically stays on board during sight-seeing tours, days at sea will be no problem.

—THE SHIPS AND PORTS— OF CALL

QEII

The *Queen Elizabeth the Second* is less of a liner, more of a town. When carrying her full complement of passengers, she has a population of over 3,000, including 1,000 crew. She generates enough power to supply the whole of her home port of Southampton. She has 4,500 square yards of deck space, half as much again as the first *Queen Elizabeth.* She is nearly 1,000 feet long, and displaces over 67,000 tons. The biggest problem, one might say almost the only problem for her passengers, is finding their way around such a collossus. It is as though you had just moved to somewhere you did not know, and had trouble remembering the way to the corner shop. In the *QEII*, the corner shop is a branch of Harrods, indeed the only branch of the Knightsbridge department store.

During the summer months, the *QEII* is the fastest passenger liner afloat, cruising, in the more correct sense of the word, at 33 miles per hour. She has a tight schedule, ploughing the Atlantic back and forth between Southampton and New York, a five-night journey in each direction, with precious little turnaround time at either end.

As passengers are out of sight of land for all but the first and last days on board, extraordinary efforts are made to keep them amused. The *QEII* carries two big bands, and several other groups, for non-stop evening entertainment. There are six bars, a huge cinema, a library, a card room, a casino and even a computer room where you can learn the rudiments of using one. Every conceivable activity involving physical exercise is catered for. As the weather, particularly in the Atlantic apart from mid-summer, can be unfavourable, a glass dome floor (the Magrodome) has been laid above the Lido swimming-pool and dance floor. Fully retractable, the Magrodome allows the Lido to be used in any conditions. Jet-lag is entirely avoided by an adjustment in time of one hour each night, which is in your favour when travelling west.

If the extra hour tempts you to stay up even later, you may suffer from a new phenomenon – boat lag, agreeable, but exhausting.

Apart from treating the usual symptoms of over-indulgence, the *QEII*'s doctor will give passengers who require it an injection against sea-sickness which works in almost every case. While the Atlantic can be rough, especially on the winter crossings which link Southampton with the New York cruise programme, the *QEII* is extremely stable, sailing through storms that would force many other ships to change course. On one occasion, during an exceptional gale, the Captain's cocktail party went ahead as scheduled, and the Captain was patiently entertaining a lady from the Rockefeller family. 'Tell me Captain', said Mrs Rockefeller, 'if the weather gets any worse, will you call for help from our Coastguard ships?' 'Madam', said the Captain, 'if the weather gets any worse, it will be the Coastguard who will be asking for help from us.'

New York

When Superman rescued Lois Lane and a rather bent helicopter (courtesy of Pinewood's special effects), it was one of the last occasions on which the Pan-Am landing pad was used in earnest. Arriving by helicopter in New York on a windy day was once an adventure, with the machine being buffeted by winds between higher buildings on either side, but the compensations were, and are, enormous. They may not offer the sustained anticipation of the dawn approach of the *QEII*, sailing past the Statue of Liberty and Ellis Island, where the poor immigrants waited and hoped for a place in the promised land, but the impact of the view from the air stuns the senses. Nowadays the favoured landing point is at the southern tip of Manhattan Island. As the helicopter descends, you see first the incredible twin towers of the World Trade Center and beside it the concrete and glass of Wall Street glistening in the sun. In the distance are row upon row of skyscrapers – all shapes, all sizes – whose very

existence seems a dangerous repudiation of the laws of gravity.

The World Trade Center can boast the world's fastest lift, which takes less than a minute to climb 1,350 feet. The view from the enclosed observation centre is remarkable – as much as 80 or 90 miles on a clear day – but reputations die hard, and the Empire State Building still retains its universal popularity as the one skyscraper everyone must climb. Its lifts are old-fashioned, its offices not far short of a slum, it is eight stories shorter than the World Trade Center but, somehow, it keeps pulling in the crowds, helped by a fund of extraordinary stories. Once a light aircraft collided with its top; on another occasion a woman, bent on suicide, jumped, only to be blown back in by the wind several floors below. As you must queue for tickets then queue again for the lift, arriving at nine o'clock in the morning is the only way to avoid a long wait.

Actually, the best view of Manhattan is from the observation platform of the lower, but much more central, RCA building. A

View of New York from the Empire State Building

World Trade Center

short walk away, the Radio City Music Hall has had something of a revival. It was here in the 30s and 40s that big stage shows, sometimes broadcast coast to coast when radio was king, pulled in the crowds, helped by the amazingly slick dancers called the Rockettes. The extravagant decor of the interior is unbelievable, and you can go backstage as part of a tour of the Rockefeller Center, reached by way of the Avenue of the Americas – the street between 5th and 7th Avenue, which New Yorkers stubbornly insist on calling 6th.

Broadway, the mecca of every young American actor or actress, is a rather seedy area of the city, centred on Times Square, the haunt of drug-pushers and prostitutes. However, the theatres on its surrounding streets still flourish, so much so that it is almost impossible to obtain, at short notice, tickets for any show in fashion. In comparison with London, they are also hugely expensive.

There are, though, other equally effective ways of spending money. Macy's, on Broadway itself, claims to be the world's largest department store and has a prodigious range of goods. Depending on the prevailing exchange rate, prices will either be extortionate or simply expensive, but it is not as expensive as Bloomingdale's, on 3rd Avenue, which is still the leader of fashion for every smart household in the city.

New York is at its most pleasant on a Sunday in the agreeable temperatures of spring and autumn. In Central Park, if you've a mind to, you can watch five deadly serious games of baseball conducted, simultaneously, on a huge pentameter, or you can simply dodge the roller skaters or the joggers. In Chinatown, home of 200 restaurants, you can see the little Chinese children in their Sunday best, on their way to visit venerable grandparents. From Greenwich Village, a muddle of little streets and off-beat shops, of Italian delicatessens and student basement flats, everyone seems to head for Washington Square. Here, you can really let your hair down and play chess, like Spassky or Fischer, on the concrete boards, or sway to the music of half a dozen groups from rock to reggae. Every Sunday in summer, a wizened old man arrives, after lunch, bent double under an upright piano which he places in the same spot each time, tunes, and then plays with breathtaking skill for a couple of hours. When he gets up to go, no one offers to help him, no one knows who he is, or where he lives. But then, this is New York.

The risks of being attacked in New York have been greatly exaggerated. Although some areas, such as Harlem, are dangerous all the time and others, such as Central Park, precarious at night, only tourists on foot and on their own are particularly vulnerable. Reduce the risk: avoid bulging wallets and expensive jewellery. If you use the subway, which is by far the fastest means of travel in a city of perpetual traffic jams, keep to the more crowded central cars.

The helicopter journey from Kennedy airport into New York, which takes 15 minutes, offers visitors a speedy and exciting entrance on to the stage of this most theatrical of cities. There are, however, some disadvantages. First, the helicopter leaves from the TWA terminal, which involves a bus ride across the airport, unless you flew TWA. Second, the World Trade Center helicopter terminal is quite a way from most of New York's hotels and is closed at weekends. Third, you can only take quite small items into the helicopter with you; everything else has to go in the hold and unloading baggage from a helicopter can be as slow a business as unloading it from an airliner.

HOTEL Grand Hyatt

Within walking distance of many shops and theatres, located on the evocative 42nd Street close by Grand Central Station, the Grand Hyatt greets its guests with a stepped waterfall, flowing past spectacular statues and clusters of greenery. Where it has the edge over its rivals is in its exclusive Regency Club, two secure floors of the hotel set aside for richer or favoured clientele, offering a private lounge and breakfast room, and every conceivable service for the hard-pressed businessman or the flagging tourist. If there is a ticket to be had for a top Broadway show, the Hyatt's contacts will get it for you.

Astor

A maiden voyage up the Amazon as far as Manaus, nearly 1,000 miles from the sea, plus regular departures from Leith and Dover, make this new luxury ship *Astor* of special interest to British passengers. In 1987, the *Astor* also cruises to the Arctic glaciers of Spitzbergen, and later to the phenomenal white world of Greenland and the aptly named Cape Farewell. Later in the year, *Astor* visits the exotic islands of the Indian Ocean.

Ocean Islander

For those who dislike the anonymity of really large cruise ships, here is the answer: all the outstanding comforts of a first class liner exquisitely contained in a vessel of only 5,000 tons which carries a maximum of 250 passengers. A ship this size is practically your private yacht, slipping into tiny ports and secluded waters, yet providing a casino, beauty salon, disco, swimming pool, sauna and air-conditioned cabins. The *Islander* spends the summer in Scandinavia, sailing out of Copenhagen, with voyages around the Baltic and up the coast of Norway. On the cruise towards the midnight sun, the fjords are fabulous: more than 100 miles up the Sognefjord to take a ride on the incredibly steep Flam Railway; and on to Geirangerfjord with its stupendous scenery. Then in winter, the *Islander* moves to the Caribbean cruising out of Antigua and among the Grenadines.

Royal Viking

There can be no better way to see the Baltic than on board one of the Royal Viking fleet, whose Scandinavian officers know every inch of the waters. It does not matter which of their three ships, the *Star*, the *Sea* or the *Sky*, you choose, for they are equally superb.

Royal Viking achieved this quality by cutting their ships in half, and inserting a new centre section into which they have placed the very latest design in cabin and restaurant accommodation. The result is remarkably successful; there are seemingly

Royal Viking Star *off the Swedish coast*

endless corridors like some trick of perspective, and, behind every door, beautifully finished cabins with full-size baths, fine decor, incredibly comfortable beds, and service to match. Sheets, pillow cases, bath towels, hand towels, even face flannels, are changed every day. You can have the full range of restaurant meals served in your cabin, and a steward is on call day or night.

If you do reach the restaurant which, naturally, is single sitting, a formidable range of mouthwatering dishes is offered at every meal, served with great style and attention by Italian or Spanish waiters. Should the ship's staff be tipped off that you have an anniversary whilst on board, be it marriage or birthday, a retinue of maitre d's and half an orchestra will accompany the arrival of a huge, celebratory cake.

The Royal Viking restaurants have another considerable distinction: they have been constructed with huge picture windows, so that passengers have a superb view of passing ships or scenery without having to interrupt their meals. Nothing is better than when a Viking ship passes through the Kiel Canal, unquestionably the most exciting way to enter the Baltic from the North Sea. The Canal, which was opened in 1885, was widened and deepened between 1909 and 1914 on the orders of the Kaiser, to allow the passage of battleships into open sea, and so avoid his Navy being bottled up by the British in the narrows beyond Copenhagen. For a ship of 28,000 tons and 83 feet wide, it is, however, only just wide enough and, at times, you feel you are taking tea in someone's living room, so close are the houses on the river bank.

Copenhagen

The Danish royal family are rather less remote than in some other Kingdoms, which is probably why even when they are in residence they do not object to tourists at the Amalienborg Palace, though, of course, you

Tivoli Gardens, Copenhagen

cannot exactly stroll through their sitting room. The Crown jewels are kept behind plate glass at another Palace, the Rosenborg, where you can see the extraordinary pearl-studded saddle of Christian IV, which, no doubt, came in handy as a source of credit at country inns after he had been separated from his courtiers while hunting. The symbol of Copenhagen, Hans Christian Andersen's little mermaid, is better seen on a postcard than from a boat on a trip around the harbour. Far more significant, if you are seeking something symbolic, is the Resistance Museum, which records how the city reacted to Nazi occupation during the Second World War.

What rescues Copenhagen from potential mediocrity as a place to visit is the Tivoli, still, despite Disneyland and Disneyworld, the most famous fairground of all. Open only during the summer months, the Tivoli has an extraordinary range of diversions, and is the only pleasure park where you can be hanging on, grimly, on the roller-coaster one minute, and the next sitting sedately listening to an open-air symphony concert. For family entertainment, or romantic restaurants among fairy lights, the Tivoli is impossible to beat.

Oslo

Situated under the guns of the Akershus fortress at the end of a spectacular fjord, Oslo not only has pleasing walks but sensational museums, three of which are amongst the world's best. Overlooking the great fjord, where the Vikings may well have launched their ships on their way to rape and pillage on some English shore, a huge museum houses three of the ships which survived. One of these, the most famous, is the Oseberg ship, with its unique collection of artefacts from the days when the Vikings struck terror in every coastal town in northern Europe.

The Vikings may have sailed the Atlantic – they certainly reached Greenland – but not on a raft of balsa wood. Thor Heyerdahl proved such an epic voyage could be done.

In 1947, he crossed the Pacific from Peru to Polynesia, a journey of some 5,000 miles, on a raft called Kon-Tiki, perhaps the most famous piece of non-motorised transport in the world, which now has pride of place in another Oslo museum close by.

In many ways the most interesting of the three museums is the Folklore Museum, an incredible collection of wooden houses and their contents, brought to Oslo from every part of Norway, and providing a vivid picture of Norwegian life through the centuries. Two of the most interesting buildings are an ancient chemist's shop and a sweet shop, where you can buy sweets made to recipes that children loved long, long ago.

Stockholm

Not even Venice can match the sweeping grandeur of Stockholm's waterways, seen at their best in the midnight sunset of a Scandinavian summer. The city was much smaller, consisting simply of what is now Gamla Stan, or the Old Town, tiny courtyards and cobbled streets, when Sweden could claim to be a great power. The best examples of Sweden's bellicose past can be seen in the Vasa Museum on the island of Djurgården, which contains the warship reclaimed almost intact from the harbour where she sank mysteriously in 1628. On the same island is the Skansen, an amusement park with one of the best ghost train rides anywhere, and a perpendicular steel tower up which a circular viewing platform rises for a wonderful view over the bridges and broad waterways of the city.

Helsinki

Devastated by fire in 1808, Helsinki was re-designed and rebuilt, with perfect symmetry, by a German architect, Karl Engel. His work is seen at its best in Market Square, near the harbour, with its statue of Havis Amanda, the sea goddess who represents Helsinki rising from the waves. However, Helsinki has its own home-grown architecture, too – the dominant Protestant Cathedral, and the Finlandia Concert Hall with its magnificent acoustics. The Finnish creative genius can also be seen in its craftwork, ceramics, jewellery, textiles and glass, in a city that comes to life in the summer after a winter of almost perpetual dark.

Leningrad

The only way to see Leningrad in comparative comfort is from a cruise ship, returning each evening to escape the regimented hotels and mediocre restaurants with service that is positively stalagmitic. The port officials alternate between aloof politeness and nit-picking nonsense, and often delay the start of a tour for no apparent reason. Expect to be taken, first, to a hard-currency department store, where choosing, paying for and collecting goods is a bureaucratic nightmare, but where the credit card slip makes an unusual souvenir. Be prepared for bumpy car rides, as holes in the road are a feature of Leningrad, there being little pressure to repair them because only the party faithful have motor cars. Intourist can lay on a car or a bus to the former Czarist Palace of Petrodvorets, with its slow-turning animal fountain, the delight of children, and its fantastic formal gardens with statues of gold. An evening at the theatre can be a magnificent spectacle, especially if the visiting attraction is a troupe from Georgia, whose incredible repertoire includes a dance through a cascade of knives thrown with unerring accuracy into the floor, which is so splintered after each season that a carpenter has to re-lay half the planks.

Although it will be little short of an endurance test, you cannot afford to miss the Hermitage Museum, where you are led, almost at a trot, by a glum Russian guide through a veritable treasure house of European paintings – including one of the largest collections of French Impressionists in the world – historical and artistic exhibits. The Hermitage itself, once the famous Winter Palace, is an unrivalled work of art, whose storming, signalled by the mutineers in the cruiser *Aurora* still anchored in the Neva, launched the Russian Revolution.

Gardens of the Palace of Petrodvorets, near Leningrad

Canberra

Although P & O have newer and more exclusive ships, notably the *Royal Princess*, with her complex of five pools including, O wonder of wonders, fresh-water whirlpools; and the *Sea Princess*, another all first-class liner, whose programme occasionally includes a fascinating voyage through the Suez Canal into the Red Sea, when it comes to cruising with children, the *Canberra* is superior to them all.

The standard is set by the *Canberra*'s playroom, which is vast, as big as many families' entire living area back home. It has a multiplicity of toys and games, a slide, a Wendy house, huge quantities of paints and things to do. For nine hours a day, the children are looked after by qualified hostesses.

On almost every cruise, there is a professional children's entertainer, who holds regular shows. While the adults have their Captain's cocktail party, the children get a special party of their own with the Captain called, yes, the Captain's Coketail party.

The Lido pool and the adjoining paddling pool are reserved for families, so that passengers who hate children (forgetting that they were young once) can go to one of the other swimming pools, safe in the knowledge that children will not turn up.

For older children, there is a special disco in the evenings, and on cruises with a lot of children on board – as is inevitably the case during school holidays – other special activities are arranged.

Whatever age their children, parents can be assured of eating their own dinner in peace. The *Canberra* carries, and will prepare, most varieties of baby foods. At half past five each day, a separate children's meal is provided, with a choice of menus, as good in quality as anything served on the ship.

Egypt

P & O's *Sea Princess* makes regular, if still occasional, transit cruises of the Red Sea, edging gently from Port Said down the Suez Canal, whose dues today still sustain Egypt, just as the Nile, with its life-giving water, sustained the land of the Pharoahs.

In the absence of the *Sea Princess*, the ideal way to see Egypt is to sail down the Nile herself, in the SS *Tut*, the Sheraton Nile cruiser built specially for the purpose, with a

Mural from Tomb of Horemheb, Valley of the Kings

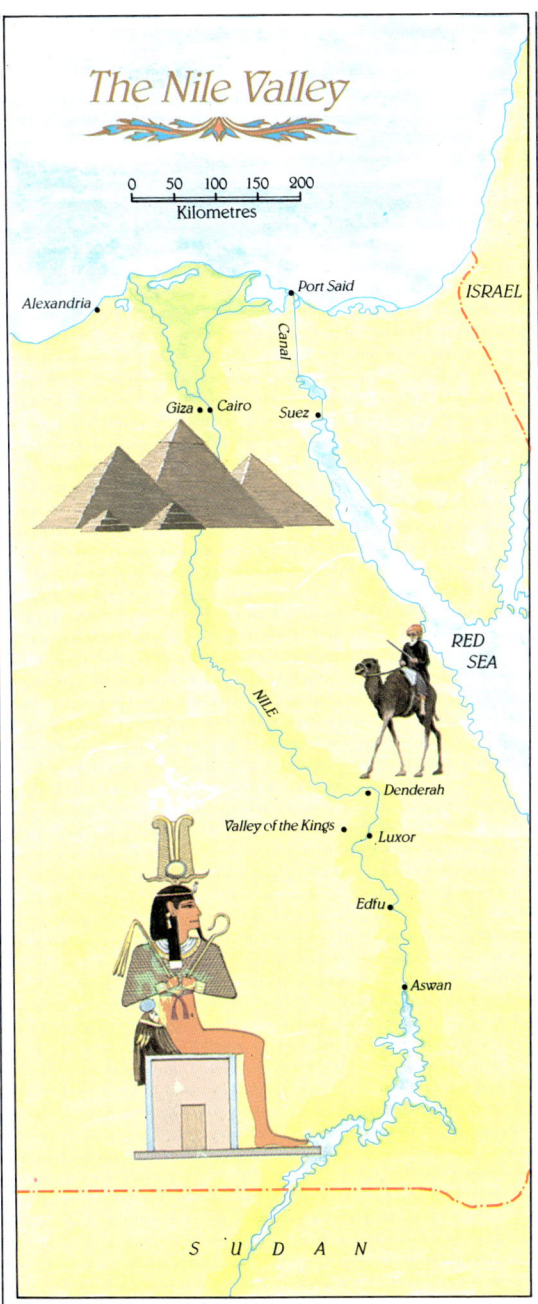

The Nile Valley

0 50 100 150 200
Kilometres

Alexandria

Port Said

ISRAEL

Canal

Giza Cairo Suez

RED
SEA

NILE

Denderah

Valley of the Kings Luxor

Edfu

Aswan

S U D A N

reach at least 95 degrees Fahrenheit and more than 110 degrees between June and September in parts of Upper Egypt. Here lies the dilemma: to visit Egypt during the winter months, roughly equivalent to an exceptionally good British summer, is to join the veritable avalanche of other tourists with similar ideas. It is bad enough at Giza to have to share the Great Pyramids and the inscrutable Sphinx with thousands of fellow visitors. But in a pilgrimage to the Valley of the Kings, which for most people is the highlight of their tour, it can mean queuing for hours.

In contrast, launched from the cool corridors of the *Tut* in midsummer for an overnight stay in Luxor, tourists can so arrange matters that they have the tomb entirely to themselves. This does not require an entrée with the Egyptian Department of Archaeology, simply an extremely early departure across the Nile, by local ferry for only a pittance, and the hiring of a guide, without whom any tourist is certain to be swamped by beggars and souvenir sellers. Although the treasures are long since gone, carried away by grave robbers over the centuries, or carefully preserved in the museums of Cairo, the tombs are themselves an epitaph to a great yet cold-blooded civilisation, cut deep into the mountain rock by slaves who had to die to preserve the secret location of their work.

Perhaps the best way to absorb the fascinating atmosphere of Egypt is to hire a felucca, a single-sail boat in which the sail is almost superfluous, so rare is a breeze in summer, and to float up and down the Nile, at sunset.

HOTEL Cairo Marriott

On the banks of the Nile, amid the gardens of Gezira Island, the Cairo Marriott was once a palace, built in 1869 for the Egyptian Khedive, Ismail Pasha. Much of the original decor has been restored, giving the hotel an old-world charm despite its bustling, modern efficiency. The hotel has a heated indoor/outdoor swimming pool which has an adjoining restaurant (one of seven in all) offering a romantic setting.

shallow draught and two decks of luxurious, air-conditioned cabins and a swimming pool.

What the *Tut* can do is to offer a respite for the tourist in the hot summer months. Hot is a quite inadequate word to describe the temperatures which – and this is in the shade –

POSITIONING

Many of the best-value cruises are what might be called positioning voyages; those designed so that ships can move to a winter or summer base, often from the Caribbean to the Mediterranean or vice-versa. For example, to take a recent March, the *Vistafjord* sailed from Miami to Genoa by way of Bermuda, the Azores and Madeira. A few days later, one of the Royal Viking fleet left the same Miami port of Fort Lauderdale and sailed to Barcelona by way of the Madeiran capital, Funchal. The ship retraced its path across the Atlantic the following November, sailing from Casablanca to Miami by way of Las Palmas in Gran Canaria and Dakar. The *Vistafjord* left Casablanca 12 days later, sailing to the Caribbean and eventually Miami by way of Madeira and Tenerife. In each case the cost of the cruise, including connecting flights across the Atlantic, was roughly a third below the equivalent fare for a cruise in either the Caribbean or the Mediterranean. Of course, it included several uneventful 'sea' days, and the risk of bad weather, but none of the voyages passed very far north, and each of them avoided the notorious Bay of Biscay.

In at least one direction, nearly all such positioning voyages include a day in:

Madeira

The itineraries of many cruise ships are arranged so that they arrive in Madeira on New Year's Eve, an occasion celebrated by a stupendous firework display, and with bonfires spread across the hills behind the capital, Funchal, so that the ships can stand off in the bay for a panoramic view of the proceedings. It is a truly fantastic sight, with rockets launched simultaneously over more than a mile, church bells ringing in tandem, and the ships, lit from bow to stern, sounding their sirens.

The Portuguese island of Madeira is worthy of a visit at any time of year. Situated some 600 miles south-west of Lisbon, and north of the Canary Islands, it has a delightfully mild climate with magnificent displays of flowers, a veritable island garden. Measuring only 35 miles long and 13 miles across, it nevertheless comfortably absorbs its annual influx of tourists, many of whom congregate, mistakenly, around the capital, Funchal.

For a glimpse of the true Madeira, hire a car and tour the far reaches of the island, where villages dependent on farming and fishing continue almost oblivious to the march of progress, flanked by wild and beautiful coastal scenery. Do not expect to complete the circumnavigation in a single day. A rally driver would be hard pressed to achieve that, because the roads wind up and down hills and have narrow, treacherous bends.

Madeira's coastline runs steeply into the sea, offering few truly sheltered bays, and even most of those have beaches of stone or shingle. The solitary sandy beach, Prainha, is a long way east of Funchal in the furthermost corner of the island. However, the nearby, largely undeveloped, island of Porto Santo, three hours by boat or a few minutes' flying time, has quite marvellous sandy beaches and safe bathing, is never crowded and thus superior to any beaches in the Canary Islands or the Mediterranean.

Even a day in Funchal can be rewarding. Buy some wicker chairs, if you have a ship to stack them on. Sample the famous Madeira wine, the favourite tipple of English Victorian ladies, who pretended to themselves that it was not really alcohol. The vines originally came from Crete and the casks were transported on carrois de bois, bullock carts, which, nowadays, are employed as a slow, but agreeable, tourist transport. The faster carros de cesto, wicker chairs mounted on toboggans, are much more fun and skim down the slippery cobblestone streets from the village of Monte to Funchal far below, kept to a prudent pace by drivers in white uniforms and straw hats. The runs are incredibly well organised, so that a picture of a tourist on the toboggan run is often available for him to buy before he reaches the bottom. If you

Temple of Horus, Edfu, one of the best-preserved temples of ancient Egypt

wonder how the cycle keeps going, the answer is that a lorry takes the toboggans back to the top and the drivers follow by taxi.

Madeira has another distinction: a glut of physicians. Half the name plates in Funchal seem to advertise the skills of doctor this and doctor that. Many Europeans still opt to retire on the island, including, of course, doctors. . . Presumably they all end up in the cemetery, though usually at a ripe old age. It was different in earlier times, as the tombstones tell, when people were sent out from England in the forlorn hope that the climate would cure consumption, only for them to die tragically young.

HOTEL Reid's

Providing comfort in the grand manner, the hotel is located high above Funchal in sub-tropical gardens, with superb rooms and service to match. Reid's was built by a young Scot, William Reid, in 1891, and soon established itself as the last word in luxury, a hotel where not even the most finicky guests could find fault. It offers a holiday where you can be effortlessly organised, with picnic walks, motor boat excursions, gala dinners and dances and even gymkhanas in the grounds; where you can relax in perfect surroundings, lounging around one of the two sea-water swimming pools. The food is French or Portuguese, the restaurants vying with each other for superiority; for the staff, nothing is too much trouble. A hotel to treasure.

Toboggan run at Funchal

CARIBBEAN

A cruise is, certainly, the most effective way of acquiring a taste of the Caribbean in preparation for a longer return visit to a particular island. Most cruises operate out of Miami, a few out of Barbados, arriving overnight at a different island on successive days. They can also be combined with a week's stay on a particular island, for example St Lucia or Barbados. But the most attractive islands are inevitably those where a cruise ship rarely drops anchor.

Antigua

A dry island, in the climatic not the alcoholic sense, Antigua has one of the lowest rainfalls in the Caribbean. Most of the fresh water comes in tankers from the Dominican Republic, at high cost, but tourists are not subject to any serious rationing. Antigua, offering an agreeable climate all the year round, and a direct flight by British Airways, is now an outstanding prospect for a holiday. It is surrounded by a blue-green sea, transparently clear and thronged with sea creatures, which laps idly, as though affected by the warm sun, touching the white coral beaches like a lover. There are said to be 365 beaches, but no one, surely, ever had the energy to count. Further back from beach number one or 365, bending in the breeze, are palm trees weighed down by huge coconuts and dozens of other fruit-bearing trees behind.

Antigua is a beautiful place, all 170 square miles of it, and the inhabitants are friendly. They seem glad to greet visitors, if a little surprised that they should abandon their hotel beaches to explore the island. Cars, not altogether sound of wheel, can be hired, though, fortunately, the road system prevents them from being driven fast. Most of the roads wind their way along the coast, into the elegant hamlet known as English Harbour, a reminder of the island's colonial past, though the yachts there today are mainly American and the dollar largely rules. For another fix of scenery, try Shirley Heights, with a breeze to cool you while you try, without success, to work out exactly which island is which among the smudges on the

The Caribbean

horizon. Or go to Devil's Bridge, said to have been discovered by the pirate Captain Kidd, where the rock formation converts innocuous waves into roaring waterspouts.

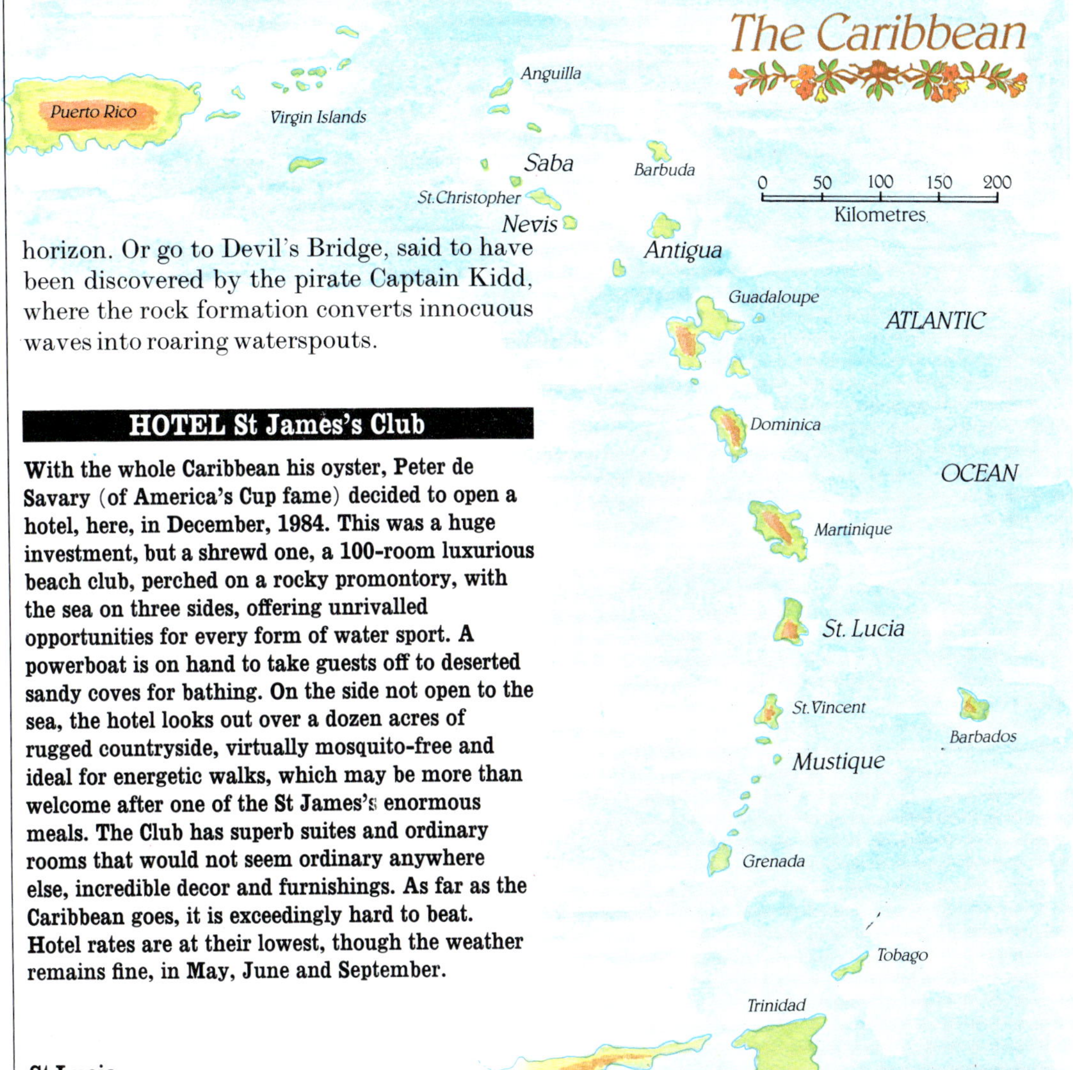

HOTEL St James's Club

With the whole Caribbean his oyster, Peter de Savary (of America's Cup fame) decided to open a hotel, here, in December, 1984. This was a huge investment, but a shrewd one, a 100-room luxurious beach club, perched on a rocky promontory, with the sea on three sides, offering unrivalled opportunities for every form of water sport. A powerboat is on hand to take guests off to deserted sandy coves for bathing. On the side not open to the sea, the hotel looks out over a dozen acres of rugged countryside, virtually mosquito-free and ideal for energetic walks, which may be more than welcome after one of the St James's enormous meals. The Club has superb suites and ordinary rooms that would not seem ordinary anywhere else, incredible decor and furnishings. As far as the Caribbean goes, it is exceedingly hard to beat. Hotel rates are at their lowest, though the weather remains fine, in May, June and September.

St Lucia

The pace of life in St Lucia is undemanding, to say the least, and visitors who can adjust to the reality have a wonderful time.

The scenery here is dramatic, with lush vegetation and volcanic hills, none more spectacular than the Pitons, twin peaks which rise sheer out of the sea by the picturesque town of Soufrière. Nearby is the world's only drive-in volcano, which has a road right into its steaming crater, with hot stones and steaming sulphur gases, but not dangerous

. . . so far. To the north lies Marigot Bay, breathtakingly beautiful, where much of *Dr Doolittle* was filmed. Here, the private yachts outdo one another for sheer ostentation and the bay echoes far into the night to the sound of on-board revelry.

The capital, Castries, is more concerned with the export of bananas than catering for the tourist, but it does have the famous Green Parrott restaurant. Avoid, at all costs, though, Monday night, when all garlanded ladies can eat free provided that they are accompanied by a male. The staff hate it, service drops from slow to almost immovable and the place is packed.

To see the beauty of the island, find someone with a boat, as many of the loveliest beaches are almost inaccessible from the shore. The next best move is to hire a jeep, in order to cope with the roads which have an eccentric camber. They are sinuous near the coast and almost non-existent inland.

HOTEL La Toc

Located on La Toc Bay and set in lush, tropical scenery, the hotel blends agreeably with its surroundings. The air-conditioned rooms are of exceptional quality, and the facilities superb – including two swimming pools, one a stone's throw from the beach, shaped, rather bizarrely, like a deformed kidney with a little island in the middle. The ice cream parlour is popular with loud American children.

Nevis

First seen, and named, by Christopher Columbus in 1493, Nevis lies off the beaten track, a tiny island that rises to more than 3,000 feet at its central point. Its scenery is magnificent – beautiful beaches bordered by coconut palms, lush vegetation and exotic bird life – and there are countless opportunities for water sports and fishing.

However, Nevis is simply too small and too undeveloped to offer any sophisticated night life. The government has wisely refused to allow any hotel development of more than two storeys, so the chance of a major multi-national company stepping in with its own hotel complex at present seems remote. No doubt, most of the visitors who come here (by way of an inter-island flight from Antigua) to avoid the hectic night life of larger islands will breathe a huge sigh of relief.

There was probably not a great deal to do when Nelson came here, two hundred odd years ago, and married, largely on impulse, a widow called Fanny Nisbet who, apart from the possible disadvantage of already having a child, was also considerably older than him. It is said that her family, in an effort to get shot of Fanny, promised Nelson a considerable income and then ratted on the deal. But they were, at least at first, a loving couple, the great Nelson, scourge of the French, having found his way to the Nisbet heart by arriving early for their first meeting and being discovered playing with her five-year-old son under the kitchen table. After an intermittent courtship, Nelson married Fanny in March, 1787. Their marriage certificate is kept at Fig Tree church. It was, by all accounts, a happy match marred only by the lack of further children . . . until Nelson met Lady Hamilton at Naples and began an affair that was to be the talk of all England and was to endure until his death at Trafalgar. A real mystery is how the Nelson Museum at Charlestown, the capital of Nevis, came by a bill, presented to Lady Hamilton, for musicians hired to play in Nelson's London house. Perhaps, like many final demands, it had been sent hither and thither in the hope that someone would settle.

HOTEL Montpelier Plantation Inn

Once a sugar mill on the plantation, the hotel is located some 600 feet up the slopes of Mt Nevis, with most of the rooms in the surrounding cottages. It has a swimming pool, a fine dining room which specialises in home-grown food, and an immensely relaxing atmosphere. Its one disadvantage, its distance from the sea, is largely overcome by running a shuttle minibus service to the superb and secluded Pinney's Beach, 15 minutes away.

Pinney's Beach, Nevis

Saba

Saba, not far from Nevis, is administered by the Dutch, having changed hands a dozen times in the course of its history. The fact that it is mountainous and easily defended, measures only six square miles, and is of no economic or strategic importance, makes the interest shown in it by the great sea powers surprising. Nowadays, it is a splendid escape from the commercial Caribbean requiring a local flight to get there.

Saba is, in fact, a paradox: a Caribbean island without a beach, a vital piece of information for anyone planning to pay it a visit. Not only is there no worthwhile beach on which to sunbathe, but swimming is precarious, because of the heavy surf. Visitors for whom beaches are a priority should look elsewhere for their holiday.

Its mountainous views, and the tropical rain forest which confronts the energetic tourist planning to climb the aptly named Mount Scenery, make this a remarkable place to visit. Some of the villages lie precariously on the rim of a volcanic crater, and one, called The Bottom, is set in the very centre, 800 feet below, with a hotel whose modestly sized rooms are filled with enormous Dutch four-poster beds.

The road from The Bottom to the top, which has the equally evocative name of Hell's Gate, was an incredible engineering feat. It passes the pocket-sized airport on its ascent; pilots who use it say that it helps to have had previous experience of landing on an aircraft carrier.

Mustique

The annual arrival of Royalty and newsworthy people has given Mustique a kudos that, perhaps, its environment does not really deserve. For when all is said and done, it is closer to a desert island than a holiday resort, marvellous if you really wish to live out in the wilds, but a little limiting after the first euphoria wears off.

Reached by light aircraft from St Vincent, which administers the Grenadines, Mustique has a tiny harbour at Britannia Bay, a general store, a handful of boutiques, Basil's Bar, which, as you might expect, is a bar-cum-restaurant run by a gentleman named Basil, and an extremely expensive hotel called the Cotton House, located next to the airstrip (too few planes for that to be a problem). The hotel was converted from an 18th-century Spanish plantation house, and certainly does not lack style. In the hills behind the sandy beaches are a number of private villas, including, of course, one owned by Princess Margaret, called Les Jolies Eaux, or Pretty Waters. Its site, on the southern end of the island, was given to the Princess in 1960 as a wedding present. On its own headland, with a steep drop to sandy coves on either side, the location is frankly more prepossessing than the villa, which has the style of a 19th-century French pavilion, without the size (it sleeps eight comfortably) or the flair to carry it off. It is approached from Britannia Bay up a rather bumpy earth road, with unpredictable pot holes; the entrance is marked by a pair of miniature square lodges, complete with gates. The house is well appointed, with three bathrooms for its four bedrooms, and a patio dining area overlooking the sea. A resident cook and maid make meals a relatively effortless affair. Roddy Llewellyn designed the rather rustic garden; the Princess decided on the interior herself. The decor is simple, but pleasing, and the main living-room has a large portrait of the Queen on the wall. A company called Continental Villas is entrusted with the job of letting Her Royal Highness's villa for most of the year. It has a prominent position in their brochure and is the most expensive villa they offer; no doubt anyone who rents it must love casually mentioning the fact at cocktail parties.

Ocean sunset from Basil's Bar

CHAPTER 6

FLIGHTS

Although there are exceptions to every rule, the best flight to take anywhere is almost always the first flown by an airline to a new destination. Inaugurals, as such flights are called, remain exempt from the usual, internationally agreed, regulations on what an airline can offer in the way of free or discounted seats and inflight services. They are practically never overbooked, partly because of the cost of promoting them in advance, especially to first and business class passengers, and partly because no sensible airline will risk any kind of adverse publicity about a new venture. The passengers travelling for nothing, be they air correspondents or friends of the airline, will always be progressively upgraded to a better seat than the one they expected, which will leave enough empty seats at the back of the plane to make the journey for the ordinary, economy-class passengers extremely comfortable. (Yes – it is possible to book on an inaugural flight just like any other.) In common with the posher passengers, they will be offered gallons of champagne, and certainly a far better meal than they could expect on a run-of-the-mill flight. Extraordinary efforts will be made to achieve punctuality, both in arrival and departure. The cabin staff, under the critical eye of the airline's chairman or chief executive, will certainly be trying even harder than usual.

Few of us, however, can make the flight fit the destination and/or date. No flying experience is so extraordinary, with the possible exception of Concorde, to justify changing a holiday destination simply to travel on a particular airline. Air travel is essentially a means of reaching somewhere as quickly as possible and with the minimum inconvenience; it is never, or hardly ever, as pleasant as actually being there.

Not long ago, the distinction between scheduled and charter flights was blindingly obvious to any holidaymaker who sampled both. Not only would a scheduled flight nearly always have a substantial number of empty seats, and thus possibly an improved level of service, but it would involve a fast, modern aircraft which would arrive more or less on time. A charter flight, by comparison, was frequently late leaving and arriving, was completely full, offered dispiriting food, and used fairly vintage aircraft.

The situation has changed dramatically. In fact, because scheduled airlines went through a difficult financial period when they delayed placing orders for new aircraft, they lost their place in the queue to the charter companies, whose aircraft were, for a time, newer and in many instances superior. The charter airlines also began to offer 'flight only' deals or inclusive tours with nominal or entirely fictitious accommodation at the destination, whilst the scheduled airlines sold more and more blocks of seats to tour operators. As a result, the distinction between scheduled and charter has become so blurred, that many passengers no longer know the difference. In a recent survey, only 48% of holidaymakers were certain that they had been on a charter flight; the correct figure should have been over 58%.

Charter flight catering, too, has improved substantially, with hot meals and good quality steak frequently provided on the longer

Mediterranean flights, and overall service in many cases is now excellent. Comfort is a different matter. The reason for this is not difficult to discover – the extremely small pitch of the seats: i.e. the distance between the front edges of two seats, one behind the other, in an upright position. On charter flights it is sometimes as little as 28in, compared with the pitch on a scheduled service of between 31in and 34in. In other words, there is not a lot of leg room on a charter flight for an average size passenger, and an uncomfortable journey for anyone over 6ft tall.

Although one tour operator has offered flights to, for example, Madeira, with a special section on the aircraft providing champagne and superior meals, on the vast majority of charter flights all the passengers receive the same food and sit in identical seats. If they are on an inclusive package tour arrangement, they have to take it or leave it; the tour operator does not offer them a choice of airline. On scheduled services, the holidaymaker usually does have a choice, on some journeys perhaps restricted to the two national carriers who share the routes, whilst on others a much wider selection limited only by commercial arrangements made by the tour operator.

Until the early 1970s, the options open to the air traveller were still relatively simple. On routes offering a choice, you could choose between a charter and a scheduled flight, and on the scheduled service, between economy or (if extremely rich, the fare was tax-deductable, or someone else was paying) first class.

As the price of oil rose sharply, the airlines were compelled to sell as many seats as possible to avoid disastrous losses and discounts, official and unofficial, were offered to fliers to induce them to travel. As a result, businessmen found themselves jammed in with holidaymakers, despite having paid considerably more for their tickets. It was no longer enough for them to be able to change their flight plans at the last minute; they wanted something better on board. The airlines responded with another class of travel given various names but known generally as business class, offering more space, better meals and improved service to that offered on economy class flights.

A few more affluent holidaymakers may be tempted to buy business class tickets to take advantage of the superior meals and service. On any journey of under three hours, it must be said bluntly that they would be wasting their money. Very few of the airlines flying around Europe offer more than marginal improvements in seating and the journey is simply not long enough for free drink (often extended now to the back-of-the-plane passengers in any case) or better meals to be of real significance.

On longer journeys, however, the business class takes on far greater significance. There tend to be much longer queues at check-in for larger aircraft such as the 747, so a separate check-in facility can get the journey off to a good start. The longer the journey, the more tired a traveller becomes, so improved service begins to count. Whereas on a short flight passengers can eat well before or afterwards, on a long flight they are stuck with whatever the airline offers, so a good meal is more significant. Most important of all, though, is the improvement in width of seat and leg room available, which can make all the difference after many hours in the air.

Another plus may be the free taxi to the airport which some airlines offer business-class passengers.

However, all the airlines have been careful not to narrow the gap between business and first so much that the first-class passenger begins to wonder whether his ticket is worth the extra money. If you can afford – and of course very few people can – to travel first-class at your own expense, on long flights it can enable you to arrive relatively fresh, and transform your holiday. Many passengers travelling economy over long distance are so exhausted on their arrival that the first few days of their holiday are effectively ruined.

What first class gives you, above all, is space – five times as much, at probably five times the price – then a superbly comfortable seat, never more than two abreast; a cabin you can move around in; toilets without long queues; a cabin attendant by your seat at the first touch of a button.

In addition to space and comfort, first class offers food and drink of the very highest quality. Take a Cathay Pacific flight to Hong Kong, for example: before take off you will be offered an initial glass of vintage French champagne, Charles Heidsieck 1976 Brut, with cashew nuts to sharpen your appetite. The meal starts with a choice between lobster Parisienne, smoked salmon, Parma ham or goose-liver pâté. For main course, you might be offered Châteaubriand Bordelaise, or grilled salmon steak, or chicken Mandarin, accompanied by a Pouilly Fuissé or a Château Batailley claret. Next comes cheese, then fruit, then a choice of desserts, coffee and Hennessy XO cognac. That was lunch. Dinner is equally exotic, and starts with caviare. The meals are served on delightful porcelain plates with beautiful cutlery, and your glass is refilled every time you look at it. The food is individually cooked, and the dishes devised and prepared by leading chefs.

After you have eaten such a stupendous meal, you may well feel an urge to sleep. On nearly all long-haul flights, a first-class ticket guarantees you a full-length sleeper seat on which you can stretch out, wrapped in blankets, with your feet in comfortable over-socks, and the lights blacked out by a blind-fold. A few airlines, including the Phillipines service to Manila, offer, for still more money, the even greater luxury of going upstairs to bed on a 747, where the cabin is divided into little curtained cubicles; what is more, you are not required to wake up for landing or take-off in transit.

In a similar upstairs lounge of the 747, Virgin Atlantic have produced a luxurious first-class cabin with a mere eight seats. The Parisian namesake, Maxim's, does the food; there is a stand-up bar at the front and a lounge area at the rear.

If you are going to spend such a huge sum of money on a long-haul flight, you will, naturally, be anxious to ensure that you are receiving the very best. Travelling first class does not automatically guarantee exceptional food and service, and standards do vary surprisingly.

What seems to ensure quality is fierce competition, at its highest across the Atlantic and out to the Far East. On the Atlantic, and indeed on many other flights, Swissair have an outstanding reputation for service in first class. In the Far East, however, Cathay Pacific, Singapore and Thai International have probably had the edge on them, mainly because of the tradition of service in the Orient. Experienced travellers, asked to choose one airline, now claim that, worldwide, British Airways are difficult to beat.

Concorde

On the main operating route between London or Paris and New York, time saving is Concorde's great asset. The journey takes under four hours, and can be achieved in the daytime in either direction, making it possible to fly the Atlantic, do several hours' business, and return home, all in a day.

Concorde cruises at Mach 2, 1,300mph –

Dr Ernst Mach of Mach 2 fame

twice the speed of sound, Mach 1 – not a set of aerodynamic initials, but the link with immortality of Dr Ernst Mach, an Austrian physicist. Dr Mach was a logical positivist, that is to say, he believed only in facts that could be established by sense experience. On that basis, he would have loved Concorde, for there is no greater experience in public transport than the plane's blistering take-off, worthy of a fighter in full fury.

But Concorde has a basic problem. In order to carry sufficient fuel to cross the Atlantic, it can take only 100 passengers and, because the aircraft is only nine feet wide, they sit in seats which, while they might seem comfortable to a holidaymaker used to charter flights, are much narrower and closer together than in first class on a subsonic flight. Although in 1985 the seats were redesigned and lowered, and re-upholstered in a grey hide, to give the cabin an increased sense of spaciousness, these were really cosmetic changes within strictly limited parameters. Of far more impact, it seems, was the expansion of in-flight information from a simple Machometer to a sophisticated display that gives altitude, outside temperature and ground speed as well.

For anyone not too blasé about first-class cuisine, the in-flight service more than makes up for the narrowness of the seats. The crockery, white bone china edged with platinum and black, positively demands to be filled with caviare and it will be, accompanied by Laurent Perrier Grand Siècle Champagne. Thereafter the meal is a gastronomic ecstasy, the only difference from a top-class restaurant being that the smoked salmon is flying 11 miles above the earth and Concorde is devouring the miles to its destination at one every 2.6 seconds. You can even sample it twice on Saturdays, when under the auspices of Air Jamaica, Concorde leaves New York for Kingston, allowing passengers to fly supersonic from London all the way to the sun.

Apart from the New York run, Concorde has, alas, not been popular. London to Washington has never made money, even by extending flights onward to Miami or Dallas

Fort Worth. British Airways could only fly to Singapore in conjunction with Singapore Airlines, which led to a monstrous hybrid livery with one side in the colours of each company. The route was, eventually, cut back to Bahrain and then dropped altogether. Air France had similar problems with Washington, which they abandoned, along with the more promising route to Rio de Janeiro.

Plans to run Concorde to Australia never got off the ground, except as a one-off to Sydney to fly passengers to join the *QEII*. This has proved a successful, if unlikely, role for Concorde. Charters have transformed British Airways' use of the aircraft, so much so that a seventh, placed in cold storage, had to be brought back into service to cope with the demand. A 1986 flight to New Zealand complete with views of Halley's Comet, another *QEII* connection to Cape Town, one-day trips to Moscow, Berlin, Cairo, Lapland and Marrakesh, plus package tour legs to Barbados, Antigua and St Lucia in the West Indies, and supersonic trips around the Bay of Biscay, have all helped to bring the aircraft within reach of people for whom otherwise it might be an impossible dream.

Concorde

CHAPTER 7

SAFARI

The starting point for any serious safari has to be the Serengeti plains of northern Tanzania, covering thousands of square miles and sustaining millions of animals – zebra, gazelle, wildebeest and countless others. It is the last place to see in such numbers the wild life which, a century ago, thronged the plains of Africa. Between mid-November and early June, when lush vegetation and full water-holes can support the huge herds, they graze together in their thousands. Then, as if by signal, they begin their annual trek north, oblivious to the political frontier, towards the great Kenyan game reserve of the Masai Mara. Every step of the way they are watched by hungry predators, lion, leopard and hyena, on the look-out for stragglers likely to be easy meat.

The advantage that Tanzania, which is reached by a short flight from Nairobi, has over its neighbour Kenya is that there are more animals, fewer hunters and people, who, given half the chance, would be shooting everything in sight with something more lethal than a camera. For a long time, the Tanzanian border with Kenya was closed. The package tour industry is not yet sufficiently convinced of Tanzania's long-term stability to reorganise many of its programmes. The lack of tourists is a positive bonus, but for those who like their home comforts out in the bush, it must be said that the three Serengeti wildlife lodges are lacking some of the basic trappings of civilisation. If you want a decent bar of soap or hard Western alcohol, you have to take your own. Even at the best lodge, Seronera, deep in the Serengeti plain, do not expect gallons of water day and night, or any significant water pressure in the shower. The Tanzanian hotel industry has virtually no hard foreign currency to remedy its shortcomings, so the prospects of early improvement seem remote.

Despite all this, the wild life is superb, especially around the Ngorongoro crater. Descend by Toyota's sturdy equivalent of the Land Rover, and you may see, in an afternoon, more examples of black-maned lion than would ever be possible in the rest of Africa. The Ngorongoro wildlife lodge is located on the edge of the crater, where you can watch the sun go down and hear the sounds of the jungle far into the night.

In Kenya, avoid any kind of day excursion safari, on which you are more likely to become part of a traffic jam of Toyotas than see a pride of lions. Several days up country are necessary to see game in its natural habitat. The most rewarding starting point may well be a lodge in the dense Aberdare forest called The Ark, which is built on stilts, with a gangplank leading you over the trees to its entrance, a little like Noah's Ark may have looked – hence its name. It has rather more comforts than Treetops, rebuilt since the Queen spent her last night there as a Princess, and offers an outstanding chance to see some really rare animals. This has been made possible by creating a concrete bunker in the basement, surrounded by discreet artificial lights, and setting up a bell system in each room so that the arrival of a rare beast (such as a black leopard) is communicated to every guest – a sort of room service

Zebra at a waterhole

Elephants at a safari camp

in reverse.

Sooner or later, however, you will have to sleep under canvas on the Masai Mara reserve. At Kichwa Tembo, this need not be the disagreeable experience those who are not campers might expect. Kichwa Tembo may be deep in the African bush, but, somehow, it has managed to provide that indispensable amenity, an en suite bathroom with hot and cold running water, as well as a well-stocked and refrigerated bar, and a more than satisfactory restaurant, where, believe it or not, gentlemen dress for dinner. Only the armed hunter-guides patrolling the camp, weapons at the ready, are a reminder that a lion or a leopard could, at any moment, be only the thickness of canvas away.

Kichwa is so close to the teeming game that only a short drive is necessary to see elephant, lion, zebra or giraffe at close quarters. Alternatively, you can explore the Mara River and drop in (not literally) at the hippopotami pools on a dawn flight by hot air balloon, a breathtaking, unforgettable experience.

However well organised, the safari is certain to be an arduous affair. An ideal way to wind down afterwards is to visit the port of Mombasa, once a Portuguese stronghold, on the warm shore of the Indian ocean, where the sandy beaches are superb. The best way to travel from Nairobi is by train, an overnight journey in sleeping cars which have seen better days. Dinner on board at sunset is a marvellous, evocative experience, matched only by the train's arrival in Mombasa, soon after dawn, at the end of the single track railway.

HOTELS

Mount Kenya Safari Club

Opened in 1984, the Mount Kenya Safari Club is probably the most luxurious hotel in Kenya. Almost all the rooms are, in effect, suites, with sitting areas off the bedrooms. The bars are fashionable meeting places for Kenyan society and the brasserie restaurant is excellent.

Club Che Shale

Near Malindi, a sleepy little port up the coast north of Mombasa, this hotel consists of a central restaurant and bar complex with white walls and a thatched roof, surrounded by 14 individual cottages. The beach is a stride or two away, and what a beach – miles of dazzling, deserted sand. You can go deep-sea fishing and catch your own supper, or pick from several water sports and work up an appetite for the restaurant's fantastic seafood.

CHAPTER 8

ISLANDS

HONG KONG

Time is running out, if not for Hong Kong itself, then for a way of life which has lasted for more than a century. Western capitalism and Chinese endeavour co-exist in relative contentment, and the British colony and local businessmen have prospered to such a staggering extent that skyscrapers seem to spring up overnight. After dark, the skyline of Hong Kong Harbour is a miniature Manhattan, lit up like a Christmas cake. During the day, the harbour is a traffic jam of ferries, cargo boats and junks, symbols of the throbbing vitality of Hong Kong.

Deep beneath the harbour is a road tunnel and the welded tubes of the Mass Transit Railway, but for nostalgia, the Star Ferry is the only way to cross. It is still the cheapest example of public transport in the world, though no longer jam-packed at rush hours, when the 'foreign devils' (as the Chinese describe all outsiders) had to ride on the more expensive upper deck. The ferries berth, be it on Hong Kong island or mainland Kowloon side, at quite a pace, the skill of the pilot and the securing lines, caught by wizened old Chinese labourers, preventing a bump. Once tied up, the bows crash down like a drawbridge and the people pour off. No sooner have they walked up one ramp, than the gates open and another tide of humanity surges down the opposite ramp, spurred on by the shrilling bell that indicates the gates closing behind them. So it goes on, turn and turn about, all through the day.

The best view on the island is from the Peak (Mount Victoria), served by an almost perpendicular railway, the Peak Tram. From the top on a really clear day you can see almost to China, or pick out the dozens of tiny, uninhabited islands that mark the outer reaches of the colony. On its journey, the Tram stops at quaint little stations, where hardly anyone seems to get on and off; but with the cost of a flat or house on the fashionable Peak, having a station thrown in for good measure does not seem too much to ask.

Not far from the terminus of the Peak Tram, a ceremony takes place, courtesy of Jardine's, whose trading empire has been one of the symbols of Hong Kong's prosperity. Every day, at precisely twelve o'clock, the ceremonial 'noon' gun is fired so that citizens of Hong Kong can set their watches. It can be heard two or three miles away, so visitors who want to see the ceremony will be well advised to do so with their fingers firmly in their ears.

On the far side of Hong Kong island is Stanley Market, brilliant for bargains, especially haute couture fashion, much of which is made in Hong Kong. Whether the machinists keep going past the end of an order and the overspill finds its way to the market, or whether these are the goods rejected by perfectionist buyers for the big fashion houses, no one knows or cares. The prices are incredibly low for what, to all intents and purposes, is the genuine article.

In the lanes behind the posh hotels on the business side of the island, the goods on offer are anything but genuine – 'Gucci' and 'Hermes' handbags and other leather goods run up locally by ingenious entrepreneurs and

HOTEL The Mandarin

The Mandarin is consistently voted the best hotel in the world. Its attention to detail, its impeccable luxury, its courteous staff, its effortless ambience are, indeed, almost impossible to match. From the moment its customers are met at Kai Tak airport, in the hotel's vintage Rolls or one of the fleet of large Mercedes, they are cocooned in a world in which their every desire will somehow be catered for. Guests do not check in at the Mandarin; they are met on the steps by an assistant manager and escorted straight to their rooms. Their likes and dislikes, placed on computer during their previous stay, will have already determined the small details in their accommodation, down to their preference in soap.

Only a stride or two away from the Star Ferry terminal on Hong Kong island itself, many of the Mandarin's magnificent 54 suites offer a panoramic view of the harbour. They are exquisitely furnished, each with not one, but two, marble bathrooms, with a range of toiletries that would do justice to a courtesan's boudoir. The towels are so thick that carrying more than one at a time is an effort. Freshly laundered dressing-gowns have such an air of opulence that it is necessary to give guests a gentle reminder that they are not keepsakes of the visit.

Breakfast in one of the larger suites is an occasion to savour: it is wheeled in by waiters with due ceremony, having been individually prepared down the corridor. Every whim of the guest can be catered for, whether it is simple bacon and eggs or a four course banquet.

Some guests become so enchanted by the 24-hour room service, whose speed, even in the middle of the night, can be quite astonishing, that they rarely venture into the rest of the hotel. Unless, that is, they manage to work up a particularly large appetite in the glass-roofed indoor swimming pool, laid out in the style of an ancient Roman bath. Then they may discover that the Mandarin has an outstanding Chinese restaurant, and, on the 25th floor, a superb French restaurant, Pierrot, which could grace the most elegant avenues in Paris.

Tucked away among the hotel's broad selection of agreeable bars is the Chinnery, where, whisper it, women are not allowed. It is a prohibition rarely challenged, because the Chinnery's entrance is close by the gentleman's toilet, not a particularly likely location for inquisitive lady guests. Those that brave its portals have been known to stop the soft murmured conversation in its tracks. The leather and wood of the Chinnery somehow subdue all sound, and the barman changes ashtrays without the slightest suspicion of a squeak.

Master bathroom of the Mandarin Suite

The Star Ferry – symbol of old Hong Kong

sold, illegally, for a fraction of the price. Further up the hill are shops full of mysterious Chinese vegetables; others display monkey's tails and other alleged aphrodisiacs for the delectation of their customers.

For bargains, forget electrical goods, which in any case are more likely to have been imported from Korea or Japan. Concentrate on products in which time and skill are paramount. Take, for example, a suit made to measure. Although there are many competent tailors, for quality and reputation one stands out – Sam, who owns a shop which tailors more concerned with appearances than with keeping overheads low would probably reject as a corridor. The thought might occur that possibly more of the world's dignatories and very important personages have been seen without their trousers in Sam's little hideaway off the Nathan Road, Kowloon side, than anywhere else. Sam keeps their correspondence in an album, including a letter from 10 Downing Street in which Mr Denis Thatcher explains how the two shirts dispatched by Sam which were buttoned on wire hangers, unfortunately triggered off the security system, and that, after the Bomb Squad had finished with the shirts and declared them safe, they were no longer fit to be worn. Truly a story worthy of the pages of Denis's Diary in *Private Eye*.

Also on Kowloon side is a market where few foreigners venture on their own simply because of linguistic difficulties. Here, the prices, being mainly pitched at local Chinese, are astonishingly low, especially for children's clothes. Bargaining is all part of the game, interrupted only by the deafening noise of a jumbo jet passing overhead on its way to Kai Tak Airport.

By now, it must be time for tea in the lobby of the famous Peninsula Hotel nearby, where the orchestra plays and the fans whirl, as the people watch who is with whom, guess the gossip and start the scandal, just as they did in the great days of the Empire. Soon it may all be gone: savour it while you can.

A Hong Kong market

Excursions to China

No visit to Hong Kong would be complete without a trip into China. Apart from major diversions by air to Shanghai or Peking, where you can now stay in a luxury hotel built alongside the Great Wall itself, the most interesting excursion is a day trip into Zhongshan province. The route to the border is by way of a hydrofoil, which weaves its way past the desolate outer islands of Hong Kong, on an hour's run to the Portuguese enclave of Macao, a pleasing anachronism with an immeasurably seedy casino. The visit to China begins at nearby Cuiheng village, celebrated as the home of Dr Sun Yat-sen, the revolutionary and humanitarian, who engineered the downfall of the Manchu rulers of China but was too unworldly to maintain power himself. His house is now a fine museum. In the town of Shiqi, the little shops sell superb jade at a fraction of Hong Kong prices. Even this part of China is largely undeveloped: the bicycle is almost the only concession to the 20th century, and tiny junks ply their trade on the Qijiang River just as they did centuries ago.

MALDIVES

The islands lie 400 miles south-west of Sri-Lanka and have a brilliant beauty which rivals any place in the world. Deserted beaches of coral sand, little lagoons of translucent water, shimmering in the sun, abound in the Maldives, where the pace of life is lingeringly slow. Of the 40 or so islands organised for visitors, Fiha-Lhohi probably has the most to offer in terms of beaches and scenery, but Kani, a quick speedboat ride from the airport, provides much more to do.

HOTEL Kudahithi

It would be difficult to find anywhere more exclusive than this, a hotel which takes only ten guests, who, apart from the staff, one to every visitor, have the island of Kudahithi entirely to themselves. The accommodation consists of five bungalows with remarkable baths designed like giant clams. The use of a speedboat is included in the quite considerable price.

Besakih Temple, Bali

BALI

They say Bali is not what it once was, the most beautiful island on earth, scarcely touched by the contagious hand of tourism, but although Bali (one of the smaller Indonesian islands, north west of Australia) now has its tourist beaches – and a few tourist buses – they are easily contained in the south of the island. The more adventurous visitors can hire a jeep and disappear into a world which has scarcely changed over the centuries, stumble across weddings with beautiful girls garlanded with flowers; or be confronted by a cremation, which takes place in a wooden tower, but in the Balinese way of things, is also a joyous event. At Mas, the wood carving centre has some tempting pieces (often bought more cheaply on the beach) but beware, they may split in a more humid atmosphere. The antique shops at Celuk, too, should be treated with some suspicion, as most of the genuine examples were bought by tourists of an earlier vintage. The pictures by local painters at Ubud are a more promising investment. Tampaksiring boasts of a holy spring and a shrine dating back to the 10th century but every village has its little temple. The biggest, and most spectacular, is at Besakih, high on the slopes of the Agung mountain, carved out of the dark, volcanic rock face; the silence there is deafening. Some of the best Balinese dancers come from this part of the island, motivated by deep religious convictions, which permeate their senses and produce a rhythmic art unsurpassed for its beauty. If something has to mar Bali, it must be the monkeys of the Sangeh forest, who think nothing of removing your fingers along with your handbag.

HOTEL Bali Hyatt

It would be so easy in Bali to ruin a place by building a concrete skyscraper, but Hyatt have built a hotel worthy of the setting. The hotel has only two storeys, a multitude of little blocks, in breathtaking, tropical grounds, with enchanting fountains and walks to tempt you back to a central complex of bars and romantic restaurants, with the warm sea lapping at the sands below.

——ANDAMAN ISLANDS——

A little piece of India in the Bay of Bengal though, geographically, rather closer to Thailand, and once a tiny outpost of the British Empire. Convicts were in the past incarcerated in the Cellular Jail of Port Blair, the main port and the centre of the Andaman timber industry. The islands are scarcely affected by the modern world. Naked pygmies still hunt for food with bows and arrows, amid an extraordinary range of wild life and vegetation. Some of the beaches have yet to be trodden in shoes. The water, beautifully warm, has an incredible collection of rare tropical fish, innocently darting within reach. You can see playful dolphins and flying fish, skimming the waves in Port Blair harbour.

HOTEL Bay Island

Constructed entirely of wood, the cheapest building material on the island, on a hill overlooking Port Blair. You go down one level to eat, two levels to sleep, in comfortable air conditioned rooms.

Seychelles beach

——SEYCHELLES——

The faint question mark concerning the islands' political stability – in 1982 some tourists on a twin-centre 'adventure holiday' got more than they had bargained for in the course of a fortnight, with a curfew in Kenya following an attempted insurrection, and a coup in the Seychelles – is easily outweighed by their stupendous beauty. The Seychelles consist of more than one hundred tiny islands, a tropical paradise with sweeping bays of vivid white sand, fringed by gently swaying palms. The most fascinating of the islands is Praslin, where the crystal-clear sea, running over the reefs, is a teeming mass of astonishing tropical fish in an impossible variety and number. The Valley de Mai, a huge, humid forest, contains the only known specimens of the coco de mer palm tree, whose fruit bears a strong resemblance to part of the female anatomy calculated to bring a blush to many a maiden's cheek. It is now an unofficial national emblem. For some mysterious reason the fruit only falls at night, and can weigh up to 50lb.

HOTELS

Coral Strand

Situated on the largest island, Mahe, on the superb Beau Vallon beach in the north-west, the Coral Strand is easily the best hotel and offers a huge range of water-based activities. It has a fresh-water swimming pool close to the beach.

Flying Dutchman

On Praslin, reached by local Air Seychelles flight or rather slower boat. The hotel is located on another fine beach and consists of a central complex surrounded by thatched bungalows.

——MAURITIUS——

Another beautiful Indian Ocean island, bounded by coral reefs, which keep the vivid blue waters within the lagoon delightfully calm. Beneath the magnificent volcanic mountain

Trigger fish and coral reef

peaks are dense fields of sugar cane, the principal Mauritius export, along with its by-product, Mauritian Green Island Rum, reputed to be lethal in large doses. Every conceivable water-based activity is available, including excursions to the nearby Ile aux Cerfs, which has the best beaches. The capital of Mauritius, St Louis, has an interesting market of local produce, fabrics, wickerwork and spices. Nearby is Sam's Disco, the fashionable hub of the island's night-life.

HOTEL Saint Geran Sun

An outstanding, luxurious hotel located in a magnificent position on the east coast of Mauritius, built on a tiny strip of land bordered by the Indian ocean on one flank and a beautiful lagoon on the other. Many of the air-conditioned rooms open out directly on to the beach. The main bar is positioned right in the middle of the large, circular swimming pool with a rather narrow access-way, so heavy drinkers need to watch their step.

—GREAT BARRIER REEF—

The islands of Australia's Great Reef stretch for more than 1,000 miles off the coast of Queensland, offering magnificent scenery, superb beaches, sophisticated luxury and, if you prefer it, quiet seclusion. Lizard Island has some of the best examples of coral and is a small, exclusive resort. Dunk Island offers a vigorous night life and some of the best restaurants. For wild life, Magnetic Island is difficult to beat, as much of it is a huge national park.

One of the most agreeable resorts is Hamilton Island, part of the Whitsunday Isles, named after the date on which Captain Cook first sailed into these waters of outstanding natural beauty. Although the Reef and its surrounding islands are protected against development, Hamilton, a former sheep station, was somehow overlooked when the territories were listed in detail. The Australian entrepreneur and former water-skiing champion Keith Williams used this loophole to acquire a long lease on Hamilton and turned it with astonishing rapidity into an international resort. The island offers a dazzling range of aquatic activities, including helicopter flights over the Reef, scuba diving expeditions, sailing on a 60ft racing yacht, barbecue picnics on deserted islets, and power boats for hire.

HOTEL Hamilton Island

The Hamilton Island Resort Hotel has a central restaurant and swimming pool complex surrounded by accommodation ranging from luxurious apartments to modest but well-equipped bungalows. In the marina just over the hill are several good quality restaurants offering a variety of cuisine. The Resort Hotel is a mere five minutes' drive from the airport, whose runway, a little short for the squeamish, allows two-hour jet flights from Sydney; the luggage, alas, does not always arrive at the bungalows with the same effortless ease as the passengers.

CHAPTER 9

THE AMERICAS

——— NIAGARA FALLS ———

The awesome power of nature created the Falls more than 10,000 years ago, when the ice age ended and the glaciers retreated. Much the best view of the stupendous flow of water into the gorge below is obtained from the Canadian side, an easy excursion out of Toronto. There are three ways to get an even closer look: one of them is in the Spanish Aero Car, so called because it was originally built by Spanish entrepreneurs in 1913. It is suspended on steel hawsers, above the boiling Whirlpool Rapids, running between Colt's Point and Thompson's Point. Next there is the *Maid of the Mist*, a ship which sails as close as she dares to the bottom of the Horseshoe Falls, where the roar of the cataract drowns the engine. This is just as well for the faint-hearted, because the engine is cut as the ship approaches the falls, leaving the sheer force of water to turn the ship on her homeward course. Lastly, for those who wish to keep their feet firmly on the ground, it is possible to descend by lift, almost to the base of the falls, and be dressed, ridiculously, in yellow oil-skins, like some bizarre cabaret turn about to sing the birdie song. However, as you enter the scenic tunnels, it soon becomes evident why protection is needed. On a terrace carved out of the rock, 3,000 tons of water cascade violently past, every second, shedding a constant spray on visitors. Some of the tunnels open out directly behind the water-fall itself, which appears as a solid wall of white water plunging into space.

The challenge of outwitting Niagara has fascinated the skilled and the foolhardy for centuries. Jean François Gravelet, the Great Blondin, was not only the first (in 1859) to cross Niagara Gorge by tightrope, he also repeated the feat blindfolded, pushing a wheelbarrow, riding a bicycle and even with his terrified manager on his back. The first person to go over Niagara Falls in a barrel was a schoolteacher named Annie Taylor, who survived. However, so many other attempts have ended in the death of the participants that both the United States and the Canadian governments have made such stunts illegal.

Niagara Falls

Niagara in winter is, if anything, an even more memorable sight, when all but the central Horseshoe Falls become crystallised into a fantastic world of ice, snow and freezing mist. Sometimes the pool beneath the Falls is frozen into a vivid ice bridge, but access is forbidden because of the risk of it suddenly collapsing.

The falls are now a huge source of hydro-electric power and, sometimes, as much as three quarters of the water flowing down the Niagara River is diverted to turn the turbines. On rare occasions, engineers effectively 'turn off' the falls altogether to study the rate of erosion. If you have seen the Falls in their full glory, it is quite remarkable to see mighty Niagara reduced to a trickle.

CANADA

The second largest country in the world, Canada has vividly contrasting scenery, a contrast which culminates in the exquisite change from summer to autumn. It is not so much a country as a continent. In its twin, and sometimes conflicting, English and French heritage, Canada possesses a fascinating contrast of language and style, echoes of a colonial past.

Montreal

Nowhere else on the fringes of civilisation can you ride the river rapids and be sure of living to tell the tale. But just outside Montreal, ten miles up the mighty St Lawrence, a jet-propelled boat can provide what even the most hardened cynic might admit to be the thrill of a lifetime. No propeller-driven boat could survive in the foaming waters, there would be no purchase for its blades; it takes a jet engine to defy the elements. And elements there certainly are: thunderous waves which pour a torrent of water into the hopefully unsinkable boat, great chasms in the rapids down which the boat plunges on what seems an unending passage to hell. Everything possible is done, of course, to make your experience dry and secure. Before departure you put on waterproof trousers, jacket, hat and boots, plus a huge waterproof overcoat for good measure and a life jacket already inflated, because if there were an emergency you would have no time to inflate it. But even with this protective clothing, the tourist remains in a twilight zone between exhilaration and panic, secretly wishing he were somewhere else, but, at the same time, living every minute of this amazing experience. Jack Kowalski, the sado-masochist who operates Lachine Rapid Tours, reckons with understandable prejudice that there is nothing to beat the ride anywhere – and he could be right at that.

Once back on dry land, most visitors will need no persuasion to retreat to the relative tranquillity of Montreal's Old Town, a quaint mixture of ancient and modern architecture – towering skyscrapers cheek by jowl with genuine Victoriana. There is even a Nelson's Column, built considerably earlier than the one in London's Trafalgar Square. In Montreal the column was erected to recognise Nelson's victory in the Battle of Copenhagen. Beating the French and their allies had great significance in a country that was a French possession until 1760.

But the French connection remains. The Basilica of Nôtre Dame, with its delightful wood carvings, is packed for Mass on Sundays, echoing what is happening in Nôtre Dame in Paris itself; appropriately enough, perhaps, as Paris is the only city with more French-speaking inhabitants than Montreal.

In the summer, jazz bands play day and night in Old Montreal's streetside cafés; the eating, the drinking and the dancing often go on until six in the morning, proving that the Montreal residents have spectacular stamina. In winter the night owls become cave dwellers, inhabitants of a huge underground world of railway stations, shops, hotels and restaurants, an integrated part of the Montreal tube system. So vast and sophisticated has it become, with even some flats built completely underground, that it would be possible in winter to exist entirely in this cocoon, never seeing the light of day for weeks at a time.

Quebec

Quebec is the only completely walled city surviving in North America. Its guns dominated the St Lawrence narrows which were once the neck of the trading bottle through which only acquiescent ships could pass. In the upper part of the city is a wooded park, called the Plains of Abraham, where, on September 13, 1759, Britain and France fought a battle which was to determine who ruled Canada. It was, for the British, a desperate last throw of the dice, as with winter fast approaching, General Wolfe had to take Quebec or retreat ignominiously towards the open sea. Wolfe decided to attack where he would be least expected, by scaling almost impregnable cliffs, and achieved his objective by a combination of luck and cunning. The French sentries were expecting a consignment of supplies by way of the river (no one had told them it was cancelled), and were easily fooled by Scottish troops speaking French – for many a second tongue. Wolfe's army reached the Plains of Abraham before dawn, to be confronted by a hastily assembled French force under General Montcalm. The French attacked in traditional columns, and were mown down by the British, firing in thin red lines, their muskets charged with double shot. The battle lasted scarcely twenty minutes, long enough, though, for both Wolfe and Montcalm to be mortally wounded.

You can see this and the six other sieges of Quebec recounted in miniature on a computerised model, complete with flashing guns, in a museum close to the precipice overlooking the lower town. Time then to concentrate on scaling the quaint and winding streets, where the houses have steep gables, French window frames and roofs of unsteady tiles that would not be out of place in Normandy.

Along the coast from Quebec, past the timber mountain destined to become pages of the *Mirror* newspaper, lies the picturesque district of St Anne de Beaupré, neat wooden houses built high against the snows, and a modern but sumptuous Catholic church of breathtaking magnificence. In summer a little tourist train winds its way along the banks of the St Lawrence, and you can take boat trips down river to see whales feeding on their way to the ocean.

HOTEL/RESTAURANT La Goéliche

The goéliche was a small schooner able to sail in the St Lawrence shallows and transfer timber from horse-drawn carts to the bigger ships waiting offshore. La Goéliche, located on the island of Orléans close to Quebec and linked to shore by a single bridge, has comfortable, well-equipped rooms and an outstanding restaurant, serving a marvellous mixture of traditional Quebecois cooking and French nouvelle cuisine.

LAS VEGAS

An hour and a quarter by air from Los Angeles, the Nevada gambling resort is a bargain in terms of accommodation. Prices are kept low to make certain that visitors are not already feeling the pinch when they visit the unending row of casinos and gaming rooms. Caesar's Palace hotel is worthy of a visit, with its incredible lobby of real marble statues and a replica of Cleopatra's barge in the middle of an artificial pond. Breakfast is a bargain, provided that you resist the temptation to play Keno, a sort of sophisticated bingo, and that you are not ambushed by the one-arm bandits on the way out.

SAN FRANCISCO

Four hundred miles north of Los Angeles, but an easy day trip by air, San Francisco deserves much more time but, curiously, receives relatively few visitors who stay long enough to do it justice. On a whistle-stop tour, cross the Golden Gate Bridge, one of the largest single-span bridges in the world and an incredible sight, ride the refurbished trams up and down San Francisco's formidably steep streets and visit (and eat in) Chinatown, probably the largest Chinese community outside Asia, with, even, its own Chinese-speaking telephone exchange.

Grand Canyon from North Rim Point

GRAND CANYON

The Mexicans called it Red River – Colorado – because of its reddish colour, but few of them had ever seen its source, far back in the Rocky Mountains, where the Grand and the Green Rivers join. From there it flows southwestward for 2,000 miles before spilling out into the Gulf of California, creating on its way, in Arizona, the Grand Canyon, one of the natural wonders of the world.

Even today, passing through the Grand Canyon, which is between 3,000 and 5,000 feet deep with the river which carved it out in a narrow, rocky gorge, full of cataracts and whirlpools, at the bottom, is an arduous, occasionally hazardous, trip, not to be undertaken lightly.

It is not mere size alone that makes the Grand Canyon an unforgettable sight. Hard and soft outcrops of rocks on the sides of the valley produce a series of red, grey and slightly green terraces. The sides of the Canyon are moulded into fantastic shapes by ravines and deep tributary valleys, with buttresses of multi-coloured rock jutting out spectacularly between them.

The Canyon is best seen by air, usually by flights that begin in Las Vegas or Phoenix, passing over arid deserts and past forbidding mountain peaks to reach the Canyon itself. The flight through the Canyon is not for anyone with the slightest twinge of trepidation when it comes to air travel. The most common aircraft in use, a twin-engined Cessna, is sometimes buffeted by unpredictable air currents which swirl inside the Canyon. Their pilots think nothing of flying with a wall of rock a few feet from the tips of their wings. It is, however, a quite breathtaking experience, with stupendous views of the jagged rock formations and the river below. The trip ends with what may well be a deliberately heart-stopping moment when the pilot banks to slip his Cessna between two peaks too close together for the plane to approach horizontal, then flies seemingly straight at the Canyon wall before climbing and turning to safety and into the welcoming arms of Grand Canyon Airport.

LOS ANGELES

Nowhere else in the world would film stars occasionally come out to greet the bus on a whistle stop tour of their homes or write to a Hollywood cartographer pointing out that his map of where they lived was out of date because they had moved; but then nowhere else would there be such rich rewards for relinquishing personal privacy. Los Angeles, a sprawling patchwork of sights and sounds, is truly a city larger than life.

The map-maker may live in Hollywood but film stars never did live there, preferring the smart, but highly expensive, residential areas of Bel Air, Beverley Hills and the Palos Verdes Peninsula; and now even the studios have moved north to Burbank. All that is left of Hollywood's famous past is a rather tatty sign, on the hills, and some footprints and handprints, set in concrete, outside Mann's Chinese Theatre on Hollywood Boulevard.

Beverley Hills is, in fact, politically independent, with its own mayor. Its residents, permanent or temporary, must certainly be economically independent, judging by their lifestyle. The huge houses, mock this and neo that, are an indictment of the architects of California, or perhaps an acknowledgement that an architect will design anything if paid well enough. If you go around on foot, private police patrols will stop you every few minutes to ask your business.

The Beverley Hills, the Beverley Wilshire and L'Ermitage hotels are among the most luxurious and the most expensive in the world. Rodeo Drive is where only the very rich can afford to do more than window shop, and includes the world's most expensive department store, Bijan, so exclusive that you need an appointment simply to get in. Owned by an Iranian, Bijan Pakzad, its clients include princes and movie moguls; the minimum credit rating is said to be an income of £15,000 a week. Customers, once they have talked their way in via an intercom and an endless series of flunkeys, are taken down to a basement bar to discuss their personal needs, and given a glass of Château Margaux '61 to

J. Paul Getty Museum; built like a Roman villa

ease the pain of purchasing. The average cost of an afternoon's shopping is said to be £70,000, but with shirts at £250 a time and ties at £100, it would not take long to reach that total.

Burbank, in the San Fernando Valley, is the centre of the film and television industry. Free tickets for the video-taping of TV shows can be obtained from the LA tourist office, or you can go on the famous tour of Universal studios, and watch bridges collapse round you, and be all but eaten by Jaws, a fictitious shark which has done a great deal to sustain the studios' profits.

Due west of Burbank and the Santa Monica Mountains is 20 miles of coastline known collectively as Malibu, which has the Paul Getty Museum of art and artefacts, probably the best in the world, acquired, literally, regardless of expense. Nor were considerations of cost uppermost in the minds of those who built the Malibu Beach Colony, where film stars and millionaires have palatial retreats on a private headland.

To the south, the Pacific Coast Highway leads to Long Beach, part industrial, part residential, and where the old *Queen Mary* is in permanent dry dock, an attraction for trippers and a none-too-comfortable hotel.

East of Long Beach is Anaheim, which few people outside LA will have ever heard of, but which accommodates two of the most famous theme parks in the world. One is Knott's Berry Farm, with three separate themes: Old West, The Roaring Twenties and Fiesta Village. Old West is certainly the best, an authentic re-creation of a western town, assembled building by building from old towns in California and Arizona. The other park is the legendary Disneyland, with no fewer than seven themes – including Frontierland, New Orleans Square, Adventureland, Fantasyland and Tomorrowland. In the summer, Disneyland is open until midnight, but becomes increasingly busy in the early evening and at weekends, when queues can be enormous.

HOTELS

Beverley Hills

A pink, Spanish-style mansion on Sunset Boulevard, surrounded by palms and sub-tropical cacti, the Beverley Hills hotel is an opulent reminder of the great days of Hollywood. The rooms are larger and better furnished than many a hotel lobby, some with open fireplaces whose fire will have been lit, long before the guest's arrival, at the slightest suspicion of a Californian winter. The food is superb, with huge helpings.

L'Ermitage

A brash newcomer by the standards of The Beverley Hills, as it opened only in 1976, L'Ermitage has gone to enormous lengths to establish itself in what, it claims, is a class of its own. The Ashkenazy brothers, who own it, decided that even Givenchy were not good enough for their bathroom toiletries, so they designed a brand for themselves, taking two years to perfect it. No-one who stays at L'Ermitage seems to have less than a suite, with Continental breakfast thrown in and a car to take them anywhere they want. Twice a month, a live concert is provided for guests by some of the world's leading musicians, presumably on the basis that if you can afford to stay there that long, you deserve something extra.

——— RIO DE JANEIRO ———

The carnival came to Rio with the Portuguese, and the first in Rio's great tradition was held in 1641 to celebrate the coronation of the Portuguese King, João IV. In the beginning it was a riotous, sometimes crude affair, unchecked until the 19th century, when the court reorganised it as a ball in the Venetian style with masks and confetti, the revellers reduced to throwing rubber lemons, filled with scented water, at one another. Had this remained the style and theme of the modern carnival, it would not now be the sensational and spectacular festival which draws tourists from all parts of the world.

The atmosphere of the carnival was changed by the poor blacks who came to Rio from Bahia, in the closing years of the 19th century, influenced by promises of prosperity. They brought with them a traditional folk music with a rhythm based on the beat of a drum. Soon it was blended into an exciting new concept in dance and choreography which became a feature of the carnival, so successfully that each district of Rio tried to outdo the rest in colour and imagination. Samba schools were created, where young men and

A samba school at Rio Carnival

women could be trained in the art and new, more vibrant, dances and rhythms tried out in private. The carnival became more and more extravagant, each Samba School parading in a series of decorated floats with themes from Brazilian history; and has evolved into the great annual event of today.

The carnival takes place in the three days preceding Lent, when commercial life in the city virtually closes down and everyone takes to the richly decorated streets. The revellers parade in exotic costumes, singing and dancing the latest machas and sambas to the bewitching rhythm of the drums. Children have their own festival, with prizes for the best costumes, and night clubs hold carnival balls with non-stop music until dawn. The highlight of the carnival comes on Sunday evening, with an all-night competition between the Samba Schools, the culmination of a year's dedication and practice by the cream of their pupils. Former samba dancers act as judges during the parade, assessing not only the imagination of the floats and the richness of costume but the choreographed steps of individual dancers. One slip can make all the difference between

oblivion and winning that most coveted of titles, Campeão da Avenida (Champion of the Avenue), announced to rapturous applause from the crowd at midday on Monday.

Despite its name, the competition no longer takes place on the avenues and streets, but in the Sambódromo, a purpose-built stadium designed by the great Brazilian architect, Oscar Niemeyer. Opened in 1984, it can seat 60,000 spectators, watching the efforts of 80,000 dancers far below. If the spontaneity of the original carnival has, partly, been lost, the creative energy remains, a massive explosion of colour and athletic vitality, of sensuous and captivating music, and a vivid demonstration of the Brazilian way of life.

Rio has a long stretch of beaches of which, incidentally, the famous Copacabana is one of the worst, plagued by urchins and beggars. If you want to stay near the centre, Gavea Beach, overlooked by the Inter-Continental hotel, is much better, and further out Ipanema Beach and the Sheraton Hotel's own private beach are better still. One of the most exciting excursions begins on the Praia Vermelha beach, where a cable car takes you to the summit of Sugar Loaf Mountain, 1,300 feet up, which has beautiful gardens and a hugely spectacular view of Rio's skyscrapers and Guanabara Bay beyond. Even more stupendous, is the view from the Corcovado, 1,000 feet higher than Sugar Loaf Mountain. The peak is crowned by the huge statue of Christ the Redeemer, whose body was sculpted by a Brazilian, and the face and hands in Paris by the French sculptor, Paul Landowski. This extraordinary co-operative effort took on a further international flavour, in 1931, when the powerful floodlights were switched on, remotely, by the pioneer of radio, Guglielmo Marconi, from his yacht in the distant port of Genoa. The final famous landmark of Rio is the Maracana Stadium, which holds 200,000 spectators, and is frequently full for a match, because football is Brazil's enduring passion. Wherever you go in Rio, on the beaches, in the parks, in the side streets, you will find someone displaying astonishing artistry with a ball, hoping perhaps to be the successor to the immortal Pelé.

Statue of Christ above Rio

CHAPTER 10

ROUND-THE-WORLD

London – Nairobi – Seychelles – Delhi –Singapore – Bali – Hong Kong – Sydney – Fiji – San Francisco – New Orleans – New York – London.

The ultimate trip: around the world by sea or air, the experience of a lifetime. There are an infinite number of possible routes and combinations, but by air perhaps this selection would be difficult to beat:

London to Nairobi – for several days on Safari;

Nairobi to the Seychelles – a short hop into the Indian Ocean with its breathtaking beaches;

Seychelles to Delhi (via Colombo) – for a short tour of India to include a visit to the Taj Mahal;

Delhi to Singapore – a superb stopover before . . .

Singapore to Bali – still an island of magical charm;

Bali (via Jakarta) to Hong Kong – where skyscrapers and ancient traditions exist side by side;

Hong Kong to Sydney – the gateway to Australia; see its majestic harbour and Opera House;

Sydney to Fiji – the unforgettable sights and sounds of the South Pacific;

Fiji to San Francisco – the Golden Gate Bridge, the trams, and side trips to Hollywood and Disneyland;

San Francisco to New Orleans – the great home of jazz: try to catch its epic carnival, the Mardi Gras;

New Orleans to New York – Manhattan, Broadway, and buildings that stretch up to the sky;

New York to London – how else but by Concorde, the ultimate flight to end the ultimate journey.

Going around the world by sea of course takes much longer than by air and can take anything from two to four months, and is, correspondingly, more expensive. Most of the major cruise companies – Cunard, P & O, Norwegian Caribbean, Royal Viking – offer a world cruise each year. In some instances, it involves a flight at the beginning and end of the cruise, to pick up the ship in New York, or Miami or San Francisco, three favoured starting points, as the majority of the passengers will be affluent Americans. They may, also, in some cases be rather elderly, as few people with jobs can afford to take off so much time at a stretch.

A good deal of the space on world cruises is taken up by passengers travelling on one section of the cruise only, flying out to connect with the ship at one port of call and leaving at another port further on. From their point of view, this has the advantage of joining a ship which does not retrace her passage, as many two or three week cruises do, and of enabling them to choose one of the more attractive sectors of the voyage. Particular favourites are sections of the Far East, because air fares to this part of the world are especially competitive, enabling cruise companies to offer attractive packages.

To enjoy a full world cruise, you do need to be a cruising enthusiast. Even if you can afford a really good cabin – and staying on board even the most luxurious ship for that length of time in cramped conditions can lead to stresses and strains – the surroundings, the crew, your fellow passengers, even the food, however marvellous, can become monotonous. Periods away from the ship on long excursions, which, of course, add to the overall cost, are the most effective relief.

Although the itineraries vary each year, most of them are fairly predictable, and generally visit Hong Kong, Singapore, Cape Town and Honolulu. However, Royal Viking broke a certain amount of fresh water, in 1986, with a cruise which included several ports of call in South America and a South Atlantic crossing. The number of days at sea is often a vital factor in influencing the level of enjoyment. Royal Viking's 106 days, for example, had 57 sea days, more than half the voyage, including a five-day stretch from Rio to St Helena (where Napoleon was exiled) and a seven-day stretch between Yokohama and Honolulu. On long ocean voyages, however marvellous the ship, passengers may begin to feel slightly restless, especially as there is little to see on the way.

Despite some snags, cruises do offer a superbly relaxing holiday, and an opportunity, for those who dislike flying, to see places that they would not dream of attempting to reach by air – not for them the excitement of round-the-world air travel.

No one of course, except, perhaps, as a publicity stunt, attempts to fly round the world without a break, pausing only to change from one aircraft, or from one airline, to another, a nightmare of transit lounge after transit lounge. The key to a successful round-the-world (let us call it RTW from now on) trip by air is the choice of stopovers, which the passenger always hopes will match the ports of call on a world cruise by sea.

Unfortunately, unless you have almost unlimited funds at your disposal, the reality is that your choice will be extremely limited. Although nearly all the major airlines offer RTW fares at extremely advantageous rates, they do so in order to fill seats which would otherwise remain unsold. As a result, heavily booked routes to, for example, the Middle East or South Africa, are rarely included; and

the tailor-made packages offered by the airlines always include North America and the Far East, areas with the stiffest competition and the highest seat availability.

Every RTW fare has booking restrictions, which usually include the following:
The trip must

a) start and end in the same country, and cannot be extended beyond RTW length (to stop crafty businessmen adding extra sections which they intend to use later in the year, and which they would have had to pay for at a much higher rate);

b) be in the same class throughout (you cannot opt for first class on particularly arduous long haul overnights, and economise on the rest);

c) be booked and paid for at least 14 days (some airlines insist on 21 or 28 days) before the first flight, although you can usually stop over as frequently as you wish (with a limit of three stopovers in mainland USA on some routes) and change your remaining flight bookings;

d) take not less than 14 days, but you can stop off en route as long as you like, provided you complete the RTW journey within 180 days (a few airlines allow longer);

e) be completed in one continuous direction, east or west (although Pan-Am/Cathay Pacific's RTW fare does allow some back-tracking without extra charge over the same route).

With a few exceptions, back-tracking and side trips cost extra.

Tickets which cover South America, the Caribbean, Africa and parts of the Middle East, areas with very restrictive fares, cost a great deal more than those for other countries. Indeed, in some cases, they are little less than the full fare that you would have to pay for a series of scheduled flights. Against that, it is possible to construct your own RTW tour on the more competitive routes, which may be cheaper than any of the official airline packages, by buying separate tickets from, say, London to Hong Kong, Hong Kong to Los Angeles by way of the South Pacific, and from Los Angeles to London.

On long journeys such as these, a comfortable airline seat may make all the difference to how much you enjoy the holiday. It also allows the option, in business and first class on the British Airway/Qantas routing, of including a Concorde flight across the Atlantic. Although first class travel is obviously a good deal more expensive, in comparison with the standard price of RTW tickets, it remains a huge bargain. Some of the airlines are beginning to realise this. In 1985, for example, British Caledonian, Malaysian and Continental, who act in tandem on RTW routes, put up the price of a first class RTW ticket by more than £1,000. The moral seems to be that when it comes to travelling around the world, if you are looking for the best, now is the time to go out and buy it.

Index of places